WORDS
TO LIVE BY

WORDS
TO LIVE BY

LIFE STRATEGIES OF THE
LATTER-DAY PROPHETS

LARRY E. MORRIS

DESERET
BOOK
SALT LAKE CITY, UTAH

Library of Congress Cataloging-in-Publication Data

Morris, Larry E., 1951-
    Words to live by : life strategies of the Latter-day prophets / Larry E. Morris.
        p.   cm.
    Includes bibliographical references and index.
    ISBN 1-57008-964-7 (alk. paper)
    1. Christian life—Mormon authors.   2. Church of Jesus Christ of Latter-day Saints—Presidents—History.   I. Morris, Larry E., 1951-   II. Title.
    BX8656.M665   2003
    248.4'89332—dc21   2003008518

Printed in the United States of America   18961-7082
R. R. Donnelley and Sons, Crawfordsville, IN

10   9   8   7   6   5   4   3   2   1

TO THE MEMORY OF MY GRANDFATHER
ALMA B. LARSEN

THANKS TO JANA ERICKSON, JAY PARRY,
AND KATHIE TERRY AT DESERET BOOK

THANKS TO MY FRIENDS AND COLLEAGUES
AT THE INSTITUTE FOR THE STUDY AND
PRESERVATION OF ANCIENT RELIGIOUS TEXTS,
BRIGHAM YOUNG UNIVERSITY

THANKS TO UNCLE HIX

CONTENTS

CONTENTS

INTRODUCTION

In 1937, right after he was called to preside over the British Mission, Hugh B. Brown traveled to Europe with President Heber J. Grant. Hugh recalled that he was one of those who had looked upon President Grant "chiefly as a financial man." He wrote, "I thought he was a great leader, but I did not feel the same towards him as I did towards President [Joseph F.] Smith."

The two men were traveling by train, and as they approached Heidelberg, Germany, they saw a huge crowd gathered on the platform. They lowered the window and as the train stopped they could hear the throng singing "We Thank Thee, O God, for a Prophet" in German.

"President Grant arose and put his head out of the window. Tears rolled down his cheeks as he looked upon those people. The train only stopped a few minutes before we pulled out again. When he sat down beside me he was still crying.

"'Hugh,' he said, 'I am not entitled to that kind of adulation. This is what they used to do for Brigham Young when he traveled from Salt Lake City to St. George. . . . I am not entitled to this.'"

President Grant then put his head in his hands and continued talking. Hugh soon realized that Heber was talking to the Lord: "O, Father, thou knowest that I am not worthy of this position. . . . I want thy Spirit to guide me in all that I do and say."

"This, to me," wrote Hugh, "showed the spirit of the man. Great humility, great faith, although he had weaknesses which at times seemed to overcome these admirable qualities. . . . I learned . . . [Heber J. Grant] was a prophet of God and lived very close to the Lord."[1]

In my study of the lives of the fifteen presidents of the Church, I have found that—like Heber J. Grant—each of them showed great humility and great faith, serving despite human weaknesses. As I have examined their own writings and the writings of people who knew them best, I have been moved and inspired by their lives. I have been particularly impressed by the way they lived and taught certain principles.

The purpose of this book is to show how the prophets, seers, and revelators of this dispensation lived true to the gospel truths they espoused, blessing the lives of others and enriching their own lives by mastering fundamental laws of life. For each Church president, I have selected a principle they emphasized—such as Brigham Young's concern with honesty, Joseph F. Smith's focus on loving his children, or Howard W. Hunter's attention to compassion. I first offer quotes from discourses, letters, or other writings that demonstrate what each of them taught concerning a specific "life strategy." I then relate stories, sometimes in the prophet's own words and sometimes in the words of others, that show how they "practiced what they preached." I believe that this combination of value-centered discussion and biographical narrative illustrates these gospel truths in a uniquely profound way.

"One of the greatest values is the virtue of hard work," said the relentless worker Gordon B. Hinckley, who launched a long career of Church service immediately after returning from his mission.

"I teach them correct principles and they govern themselves," proclaimed Joseph Smith, who once headed off a high council intent on disciplining a man accused of misinterpreting the book of Revelation.

"Do the right thing and let the chips fall where they may," stated Ezra Taft Benson, who showed remarkable courage under fire as Secretary of Agriculture.

These and the other accounts related in *Words to Live By* have given me a new appreciation for the lives of the latter-day prophets. Not surprisingly, the values they teach and emulate are closely linked to the values taught by the Savior in the New Testament: charity, humility, integrity, and purity.

As Hugh B. Brown said of Heber J. Grant, "I learned to love the man and to know something of his deeper nature."[2] As you read this book, I hope that you also will be inspired to righteous living and will gain new love for and understanding of these servants of God.

1

"I TEACH THEM CORRECT PRINCIPLES AND THEY GOVERN THEMSELVES"

Joseph Smith

THE WORDS HE LIVED BY

J oseph Smith was once asked, "How do you govern these people, these Americans, these Britons, these Scandinavians, these men from all parts of the world, all nationalities, speaking different languages, having different customs and traditions,—how do you govern them, that they live together in peace, with a common purpose, and in the spirit of unity?"

Joseph responded: "I teach them correct principles, and they govern themselves."[1]

Throughout his ministry, the Prophet continually emphasized this value:

> Here is a principle . . . which we are bound to be exercised with, that is, in common with all men. . . . This principle guarantees

to all parties, sects, and denominations, and classes of religion, equal, coherent, and indefeasible rights. . . . Hence we say, that the Constitution of the United States is a glorious standard; it is founded in the wisdom of God. It is a heavenly banner; it is to all those who are privileged with the sweets of its liberty, like the cooling shades and refreshing waters of a great rock in a thirsty and weary land. It is like a great tree under whose branches men from every clime can be shielded from the burning rays of the sun.[2]

Sectarian priests cry out concerning me, and ask, "Why is it this babbler gains so many followers, and retains them?" I answer, It is because I possess the principle of love. All I can offer the world is a good heart and a good hand.

The Saints can testify whether I am willing to lay down my life for my brethren. If it has been demonstrated that I have been willing to die for a "Mormon," I am bold to declare before heaven that I am just as ready to die in defending the rights of a Presbyterian, a Baptist, or a good man of any other denomination; for the same principle which would trample upon the rights of the Latter-day Saints would trample upon the rights of the Roman Catholics, or any other denomination who may be unpopular and too weak to defend themselves.

It is a love of liberty which inspires my soul—civil and religious liberty to the whole of the human race. Love of liberty was diffused into my soul by my grandfathers while they dandled me on their knees; and shall I want friends? No.[3]

James Arlington Bennett was a prominent New Yorker who was friendly toward the Church. As early as 1839, he had urged the creation of a self-governing Mormon community in the Northwest. In a letter to Bennett written in 1842, Joseph Smith once again emphasized the principle of freedom:

Mormonism, is the pure doctrine of Jesus Christ; of which I myself am not ashamed. . . . This, is a good principle for when we see virtuous qualities in men, we should always acknowledge them, let their understanding be what it may, in relation to creeds and doctrine; for all men are, or ought to be, free; possessing inalienable rights, and the high and noble qualifications of the laws of nature, and of self preservation; to think, and act, and say as they please while they maintain a due respect, to the rights, and privileges of all other creatures; infringing upon none. This doctrine, I do most heartily subscribe to, and practice.[4]

HE LIVED AS HE TAUGHT

"I WANT THE LIBERTY OF THINKING AND BELIEVING AS I PLEASE"

On Saturday, 8 April 1843, a group of Nauvoo Saints gathered to hear a sermon from the Prophet Joseph Smith, then thirty-seven years old. They met in the open, near the frozen Mississippi River, which had formed a natural bridge to Iowa for the previous four months. The slow spring thaw had finally nudged the ice loose, and the crowd could hear and see huge masses of ice breaking apart and floating downstream. The wind was whipping and gusting, making it difficult to hear, and the Prophet asked for the faith and prayers of the congregation that the wind would be stilled and his lungs strengthened.

Sitting in the crowd was Brother Pelatiah Brown, who, in Joseph's words, had been "hauled up for trial before the High Council" for teaching false doctrine concerning the book of

Revelation. Joseph took occasion to emphasize the importance of letting people govern themselves.

"I did not like the old man being called up for erring in doctrine," declared Joseph. ". . . I want the liberty of thinking and believing as I please. It feels so good not to be trammelled. It does not prove that a man is not a good man because he errs in doctrine.

"The High Council undertook to censure and correct Elder Brown, because of his teachings in relation to the beasts," explained Joseph. "Whether they actually corrected him or not, I am a little doubtful, but don't care. Father Brown came to me to know what he should do about it. The subject particularly referred to was the four beasts and four-and-twenty elders mentioned in Rev. 5:8—'And when he had taken the book, the four beasts and four-and-twenty elders fell down before the Lamb having every one of them harps, and golden vials full of odors, which are the prayers of saints.'"

The Prophet went on to explain that while Brother Brown "did whip sectarianism," he was mistaken in his interpretation. It was therefore best for Pelatiah, who had been called to establish a branch of the Church in Joseph's old home of Palmyra, New York, to concern himself with other matters. "Declare the first principles," advised Joseph, "and let mysteries alone, lest ye be overthrown. . . . Elder Brown, when you go to Palmyra, . . . preach those things the Lord has told you to preach about—repentance and baptism for the remission of sins."[5]

Joseph thus gently corrected Brother Brown while still honoring his freedom to think for himself.

"HE NEVER UTTERED A MURMUR OR COMPLAINT"

Joseph Smith's leadership style was particularly evident during a march from Kirtland, Ohio, to Independence, Missouri. Hearing that the Saints in Missouri had been attacked by mobs and had seen their homes burned and livestock killed, Joseph enlisted a large group to make the long trek to Missouri and assist their fellow Saints. "The expedition would take axes, saws, chisels, spades, hoes, and other tools for the Missouri settlers, as well as food, bedding, clothing, teams, and wagons for themselves. The 2,000-mile round trip would require at least forty days each way.

"Zion's Camp, as the expedition was called, left Kirtland on May 1, 1834. By the time they reached Missouri, they numbered 205 men, 11 women (wives of recruits, taken along as cooks and washerwomen), and 7 children. Since their twenty-five wagons were loaded with arms, supplies, and relief provisions for the embattled Saints in Missouri, they walked the distance."[6]

Rather than exercising tight control, the twenty-eight-year-old Prophet relied on the men to govern themselves, with each group of ten-to-twelve electing its own captain. Two men were then assigned to cook, two to make fires, two to pitch tents, two to provide water, and two to care for the horses. Each company prayed together. "We travelled like the Children of Israel," recalled Wilford Woodruff.[7]

The Prophet also encouraged love and self-reliance among the group by bearing his full share of the burden without murmuring. Said one member of the camp: "It is due his memory for me to here place on record the fact that I never, in that camp or during the trials of his later life, saw Joseph Smith the Prophet falter or shrink from the performance of any duty or undertaking that the Lord had commanded or inaugurated."[8]

Others echoed this view of Joseph: "The road was so bad that we twice during the day had to unhitch our teams from our wagons and draw them by hand. Here I saw the Prophet wade in mud over the tops of his boot legs and help draw the wagons out."[9]

"Zion's Camp, in passing through the State of Indiana, had to cross very bad swamps, consequently we had to attach ropes to the wagons to help them through, and the Prophet was the first man at the rope in his bare feet. This was characteristic of him in all times of difficulty."[10]

As George A. Smith concluded: "The Prophet Joseph took a full share of the fatigues of the entire journey. In addition to the care of providing for the Camp and presiding over it, he walked most of the time and had a full proportion of blistered, bloody and sore feet, which was the natural result of walking from 25 to 40 miles a day in a hot season of the year. But during the entire trip he never uttered a murmur or complaint, while most of the men in the Camp complained to him of sore toes, blistered feet, long drives, scanty supply of provisions, poor quality of bread, bad corn dodger, frouzey butter, strong honey, maggotty bacon and cheese, etc., even a dog could not bark at some men without their murmuring at Joseph. If they had to camp with bad water it would nearly cause rebellion, yet we were the Camp of Zion, and many of us were prayerless, thoughtless, careless, heedless, foolish or devilish and yet we did not know it. Joseph had to bear with us and tutor us, like children. There were many, however, in the Camp who never murmured and who were always ready and willing to do as our leaders desired."[11]

Though Zion's Camp was prevented by the governor of Missouri from accomplishing some of its main goals, Joseph's leadership had a powerful effect. "This was the starting point of my knowing how to lead Israel," said Brigham Young of Zion's Camp. "I watched every word and summed it up, and I knew just as well how to lead this kingdom as I know the way to my own house. I would not exchange the knowledge I have received this season for the whole of Geauga County [Ohio]; for property and mines of wealth are not to be compared to the worth of knowledge."[12]

Joseph Smith was born 23 December 1805 in Sharon, Vermont, to Joseph Smith Sr. and Lucy Mack. Married Emma Hale 18 January 1827, eleven children (two of whom were adopted). Ordained an apostle with Oliver Cowdery by Peter, James, and John presumably in the spring of 1829 (although the date is not certain). Sustained as First Elder of the Church 6 April 1830 at age twenty-four. Sustained as president of the High Priesthood 25 January 1832 at age twenty-six. Martyred at Carthage Jail, Illinois, 27 June 1844 at age thirty-eight.

2

"FULFILL YOUR CONTRACTS AND SACREDLY KEEP YOUR WORD"

Brigham Young

THE WORDS HE LIVED BY

On 21 September 1875, seventy-four-year-old Brigham Young wrote a letter to his son Alfales, who was then attending law school at Michigan University. After discussing family and local news, Brother Brigham turned to a subject dear to his heart: honesty.

> I want my sons to realize and would be glad if all the world could understand that no matter whether a man is a lawyer, a doctor, a mechanic, or indeed, be he engaged in any occupation whatever, that thorough honesty and integrity will always lead to success, influence, and respect. If a young man wishes to prosper in his profession, this is the only sure road to progress. On the

other hand, if he allows himself to be led from the direct path of honesty, either through the desire to make money fast, or, as appears to be the idea with some members of the legal profession, that in the advocacy of a cause or the defense of a client everything is proper that the law does not condemn, if he permits this feeling to guide him he will be looked upon with jealousy and distrust by those who are acquainted with his course, not to say anything about the sinfulness of being dishonest. There is no doubt but that Benjamin Franklin's motto is a true one that "honesty is the best policy." I wish to impress this truth firmly on your mind and on the minds of our other brethren who are studying law, as no other profession seems more open to this evil than theirs, that you will not forget it through all the intercourse and associations of your lives.[1]

Brigham Young frequently echoed this theme in his public sermons:

We need to learn, practice, study, know and understand how angels live with each other. When this community comes to the point to be perfectly honest and upright, you will never find a poor person; none will lack, all will have sufficient. Every man, woman, and child will have all they need just as soon as they all become honest. When the majority of the community are dishonest, it maketh the honest portion poor, for the dishonest serve and enrich themselves at their expense.[2]

It is much better to be honest; to live here uprightly, and forsake and shun evil, than it is to be dishonest. It is the easiest path in the world to be honest,—to be upright before God; and when people learn this, they will practice it.[3]

Simple truth, simplicity, honesty, uprightness, justice, mercy, love, kindness, do good to all and evil to none, how easy it is to live by such principles! A thousand times easier than to practice deception![4]

This principle of honesty meant that a person would live strictly according to the promises he had made to others:

I have no fellowship for a man that will make a promise and not fulfil it.[5]

One man says, "I have agreed to do thus and so." Then go and do it. Fulfill your contracts and sacredly keep your word.[6]

HE LIVED AS HE TAUGHT

Repaying a Forty-Year-Old Debt

Historian Leonard Arrington related the following concerning Brigham Young: "While living in Mendon [New York] in the late 1820s, he incurred two debts that went unpaid for years, one that the seller later could find no record of and would not let him repay, and one that he himself had forgotten. In 1866, having found a slip indicating he did indeed owe the debt, he instructed his son John to go through Monroe County on his way east and repay, to the heirs if the lender was no longer alive, those two debts totaling ten dollars."[7]

The Tribute of Susa Young Gates

Susa Young Gates was a prominent writer, genealogist, and Relief Society leader. Speaking of her father, Brigham Young, Sister Gates wrote: "What was his outstanding characteristic as revealed by his history and the testimony of his associates? It was *integrity*, that beautiful word, so rarely used to-day, which explains the basis of his thoughts, his addresses and actions. All other virtues circle around that illuminative trait and light up the divisions of chastity and honesty, truthfulness, probity and dependability. Other traits he had, but the flame of his directing genius and governing power appears on the mental screen and may not be altogether translated into words."[8]

DEALING JUSTLY WITH NATIVE AMERICANS

In his dealings with Native Americans, Brigham Young stressed honesty and fairness. Although the Ute chief, Walker, had initially been antagonistic toward the Mormon pioneers, he came to respect Brigham Young, who sent gifts of cattle, guns, clothing, food, and tobacco. "Tell [your tribe]," wrote Brigham, "we are their very best friends they have on the earth. We shall vary not, nor turn, either to the right hand or the left. We are their friends. . . .

"And now, Brother Walker, you have never known me to be ought but your steadfast, undeviating friend. No two faces, nor double meaning, . . . have I ever shown you, and I never shall."[9]

Chief Walker saw that Brigham's actions were consistent with such promises. "By the time of his death, early in 1855, Walker was willing to say that Brigham really had been his best friend."[10]

When President Young sent clothing for poor Indian women and children in Iron County, he stressed, "I deem it the best policy to require the Indians to pay in labor for every article, as it has a much better tendency than to bestow upon them in idleness, besides it learns them to work and to depend upon their own exertions for a subsistence."[11]

"We expect you to feed and clothe [the Indians] so far as lies in your power," Brigham told the brethren of the Church. "Never turn them away hungry from your door; teach them the art of husbandry. . . . Be just and quiet, firm and mild, patient and benevolent, generous and watchful in all your intercourse with them; learn their language so that you can explain matters to them, and make them understand you. Employ them and pay them the full and just reward for their labor, and treat them in all respects as you would like to be treated."[12]

Similarly, when Brigham heard that white employees on an Indian farm were "gambling, drinking liquor, swearing and setting bad examples before the Indians," he responded by writing, "It has ever been my aim, in all my intercourse with the Natives, to teach them by example as well as precept, and to endeavor to exercise a good wholesome and salutary influence over them."[13]

But Brigham perhaps taught honesty and honor best by battling the Indian practice of selling children into Mexican slavery. He advised the Saints that when they were confronted with this heartbreaking problem, they should "buy up the Lamanite children as fast as they could, and educate them, and teach them the Gospel."[14]

HORACE GREELEY'S IMPRESSION OF BRIGHAM YOUNG

In July 1859, forty-eight-year-old editor and reformer Horace Greeley arrived in Salt Lake City to interview Brigham Young, then fifty-eight. Greeley carefully recorded his two-hour conversation with Brigham, which the Library of Congress has called "the first full-fledged modern interview with a well-known public figure" to be published in an American newspaper.

Greeley reported that the Mormon prophet was a "portly, frank, good-natured, rather thickset man . . . plainly dressed in thin summer clothing" who seemed "to enjoy life, and to be in no particular hurry to get to heaven." Nor was Brigham's candid, honest manner lost on Greeley. He noted that the Church president "spoke readily, not always with grammatical accuracy, but with no appearance of hesitation or reserve, and with no apparent desire to conceal anything." Greeley concluded that the Mormon leaders looked "as little like crafty hypocrites or swindlers as any body of men I ever met."[15]

Brigham Young was born 1 June 1801 in Whittingham, Vermont, to John Young and Abigail Howe. Married Miriam Works 8 October 1824. Twenty-five wives, fifty-seven children. Ordained an apostle 14 February 1835 at age thirty-three by Oliver Cowdery, David Whitmer, and Martin Harris. Appointed President of Twelve Apostles 19 January 1841. Ordained President of the Church 5 December 1847 in Kanesville, Iowa, at age forty-five. Died in Salt Lake City 29 August 1877 at age seventy-six.

3

"WE ARE THE FRAMERS OF OUR OWN DESTINY"

John Taylor

THE WORDS HE LIVED BY

In June 1860, John Taylor was fifty-one years old. He had served in the Quorum of the Twelve for close to twenty-two years. In an address delivered in the tabernacle, the eloquent apostle spoke on agency and accountability:

> Are we not the framers of our own destiny? Are we not the arbitrators of our fate? . . . It is our privilege to determine our own exaltation or degradation; it is our privilege to determine our own happiness or misery in the world to come. What is it that brings happiness now—that makes us so joyous in our assembling together? It is not wealth; for you may pour wealth, honour, influence, and all the luxuries of this world into the lap of man; and, destitute of the

14

Spirit of God, he will not be happy, for that is the only source from which true happiness and comfort can come.

If I am doing right, I am preparing for thrones, principalities, and dominions, resolved by the help of God that no man shall rob me of my crown. With this view of the subject, all the outward circumstances of this life do not trouble me.[1]

This proved to be a common theme in John Taylor's sermons:

Besides the preaching of the Gospel, we have another mission, namely, the perpetuation of the free agency of man and the maintenance of liberty, freedom, and the rights of man. There are certain principles that belong to humanity outside of the Constitution, outside of the laws, outside of all the enactments and plans of man, among which is the right to live; God gave us the right and not man; no government gave it to us, and no government has a right to take it away from us. We have a right to liberty—that was a right that God gave to all men; and if there has been oppression, fraud or tyranny in the earth, it has been the result of the wickedness and corruptions of men and has always been opposed to God and the principles of truth, righteousness, virtue, and all principles that are calculated to elevate mankind.[2]

Do we wish to deprive anybody of his rights? Not that I know of. . . . Do we wish to interfere with anybody's religion? I hope you do not do it here. You have Methodists and Presbyterians and Catholics, as well as other different sects; would you want to interfere with them? I do not think for a moment that you would. . . .

But while we accord to all men the right to think, and the right to worship as they please, we claim the same right for ourselves. And then we do not want to have a set of men placed over us in a governmental capacity who do not recognize the rights of humanity; men who want to control the human mind. We want to maintain correct principles; and we want to sustain all men that do maintain them. . . .

But it is our duty to maintain our rights; it is our duty to stand

15

up for those principles which guarantee freedom to man, and we intend to do it, God being our helper; and not permit the wicked and ungodly, the corrupt and depraved to deprive us of our rights.[3]

How does God feel towards the human family? He feels that they are his children. What, all? Yes; the white, the black, the red, the Jew, the Gentile, the heathen, the Christian and all classes and grades of men; he feels interested in all, he has done so from the beginning, and will continue to do so to the end. He will do all that lies in his power for the benefit, blessing, and exaltation of the human family, both in time and eternity, consonant with those laws and those eternal principles that I have referred to: from which he himself cannot deviate.

We sometimes get up feelings about parties that do not think as we do, and do not believe as we do, and we are apt to cast aspersions upon them. Why, these are their affairs. What! would you allow everybody to worship as they please? Certainly. What? If you knew they were in error? Certainly. I would not wish to control the human mind; I would not control the actions of men, God does not do it, he leaves them to their own agency to combat with the trials, temptations, adversities and evils of every kind that are in the world, to which humanity is, or can be incident. He put within their reach, however, certain principles and would like to lead them to himself if they would be led. If not, he then does the very best with them that he can.[4]

HE LIVED AS HE TAUGHT

COURAGE IN THE FACE OF DANGER

In 1838, twenty-nine-year-old John Taylor, a convert of two years, abandoned plans to move his family from Toronto to

Kirtland, Ohio (though he had already purchased a home, barn, and five acres of land in Kirtland), and responded to Joseph Smith's call to go to Far West, Missouri. He and his wife, Leonora, were nearly penniless, but John was convinced that "God will open out the way." Within days, a fellow Saint offered to travel with them and provide provisions. Others offered clothing and other supplies. John wrote that there was "enough to last myself and several families for several hundred miles."[5]

Near Columbus, Ohio, John was invited to speak at an outdoor meeting. Then he got word that a group of men were planning to tar and feather him if he tried to speak. Others advised him to cancel the meeting, but Elder Taylor was determined to go forward. He went at the appointed time and saw that a huge crowd had gathered. He started by informing them that he was from Canada, a country that was under the rule of a monarch. But America enjoyed greater freedoms. He continued:

"I now stand among men whose fathers fought for and obtained one of the greatest blessings ever conferred upon the human family—the right to think, to speak, to write; the right to say who shall govern them, and the right to worship God according to the dictates of their own consciences—all of them sacred, human rights, and now guaranteed by the American Constitution. I see around me the sons of those noble sires, who, rather than bow to the behests of a tyrant, pledged their lives, fortunes and sacred honors to burst those fetters, enjoy freedom themselves, bequeath it to their posterity, or die in the attempt.

"They nobly fought and nobly conquered; and now . . . the flag of freedom waves from Wisconsin to Louisiana—from Maine to Missouri. Not only so, but your vessels—foremost in the world—sail over oceans, seas and bays; visiting every nation, and wherever those vessels go your flag flutters in the breeze, a hope is inspired among the down-trodden millions, that they, perchance, if they cannot find liberty in their own land, may find it with you. . . . Gentlemen, with you liberty is more than a name; it is incorporated in your system; it is proclaimed by your senators; thundered by your cannon; lisped by your infants; taught to your school-boys; it echoes from mountain to mountain; reverberates through your valleys, and is whispered by every breeze. . . .

"But, by the by, I have been informed that you purpose to tar and feather me, for my religious opinions. Is this the boon you have inherited from your fathers? Is this the blessing they purchased with their dearest hearts' blood—this your liberty? If so, you now have a victim, and we will have an offering to the goddess of liberty."

At this point he ripped open his vest, saying, "Gentlemen, come on with your tar and feathers, your victim is ready; and ye shades of the venerable patriots, gaze upon the deeds of your degenerate sons! Come on, gentlemen! Come on, I say, I am ready!"

The crowd seemed stunned. He stood erect and defiant; no one stepped forward to accept his invitation. He waited for a few moments, and then continued with his address, preaching with power for three hours.

After his message, some of those in attendance stepped forward to praise his speech—and to argue that they had never intended to tar and feather him. But John's associates knew otherwise, insisting that tar and feathers had been brought and made ready, but that the crowd had been shamed and awed by the bold words of Elder Taylor.[6]

DEFENDING THE CONSTITUTION

Right to the end of his life, John Taylor showed that he was the "framer of his own destiny." In March 1882, just a year and a

18

half after he was sustained as President of the Church, Congress passed the Edmunds Act, which prohibited plural marriage and enacted fines and imprisonment for anyone who practiced it. Many men were forced into hiding when federal officials began searching for them, leaving women and children to manage farms and livestock.

A number of Latter-day Saints were soon tried, convicted, and imprisoned. Lorenzo Snow, George Q. Cannon (a counselor to President Taylor in the First Presidency), and Rudger Clawson (a future apostle) were among those who served prison sentences.

In a revelation to John Taylor, the Lord declared that Satan was seeking "to take away the free agency of man [as] in the beginning . . . and has sought to introduce the same principles upon the earth, which principles are opposed to me, to my institutions and my laws, and to the freedom, the welfare and happiness of man." President Taylor, however, chose not to have his actions dictated by his persecutors. In his final address in the tabernacle, in February 1885, he urged the Saints not to revile against revilers— "no breaking of heads, or bloodshed, rendering evil for evil. Let us try to cultivate the spirit of the gospel, and adhere to the principles of truth. . . . While other men are seeking to trample the Constitution under foot, we will try to maintain it. . . . And as I have said before I say today,—I tell you in the name of God, WOE! to them that fight against Zion, for God will fight against them!"[7]

President Taylor then went into hiding, living for a few days at a time with one family of Saints before moving to another location. In these trying circumstances he continued to administer the affairs of the Church, as his incoming and outgoing correspondence was delivered to a "safe house" each night. Throughout it all, he defended the Constitution and the freedoms that he himself had

WORDS TO LIVE BY

been denied. He was still on the "underground," living with the
Thomas F. Roueché family in Kaysville, Utah, when he died in July
1887.

John Taylor was born 1 November 1808 in Milnthorpe, England, to James Taylor and
Agnes Taylor. Married Leonora Cannon 28 January 1833 in Toronto. Nine wives, thirty-
four children. Ordained an apostle 19 December 1838. Ordained President of the Church
10 October 1880—three years after the death of Brigham Young. Died 25 July 1887 in
Kaysville, Utah, at age seventy-eight.

4

"GET THE SPIRIT OF GOD AND THEN FOLLOW ITS DICTATES"

Wilford Woodruff

~

THE WORDS HE LIVED BY

Wilford Woodruff became legendary for his sensitivity to the Spirit and his willingness to follow it. Throughout his extensive missionary labors and Church service, he showed remarkable faith. He was therefore well qualified to speak on the subject. "Every man should get the Spirit of God, and then follow its dictates," he said. "This is revelation. It doesn't make any difference what the spirit tells you to do; it will never tell you to do anything that is wrong."[1]

President Woodruff had a similar attitude toward preaching the gospel:

> I made a covenant with the Lord, years ago, that whatever he would impress me to say, I would preach to the people. If we are

21

not able to speak to your edification, it is not because there are not truth and knowledge, principles and laws sufficient within the pale of this Church, and connected with the work in which we are engaged.[2]

In my public teaching I never permit my mind to follow in any channel except that which the Spirit dictates to me, and this is the position we all occupy when we meet with the Saints, or when we go forth to preach the gospel. As Jesus told his apostles, take no thought what ye shall say, it is told us, take no thought what we shall say; but we treasure up in our minds words of wisdom by the blessing of God and studying the best books.[3]

I have never seen a day since I have been a member of this Church, that I have felt that any man was qualified to teach saint or sinner, Jew or Gentile, the inhabitants of the earth abroad or at home, only as he was moved upon by the power of God.[4]

President Woodruff stressed that this kind of spiritual guidance is available to all members of the Church:

It is the privilege of every man and woman in this kingdom to enjoy the spirit of prophecy, which is the Spirit of God; and to the faithful it reveals such things as are necessary for their comfort and consolation, and to guide them in their daily duties.[5]

Oh! Ye Latter-day Saints, you talk about revelation, and wonder if there is any revelation. Why, bless your souls, say nothing about the apostles and elders around me, these mountains contain thousands upon thousands of devoted women, holy women, righteous women, virtuous women, who are filled with the inspiration of Almighty God. Yes, these women have brought forth an army of sons and daughters in these mountains, by the power of God, and these sons and daughters partake of the inspiration of their mothers, as well as of their fathers. . . . Yes, we have revelation. The Church of God could not live twenty-four hours without revelation.[6]

With regard to our position before we came here, I will say that we dwelt with the Father and with the Son, as expressed in the hymn, "O My Father," that has been sung here. That hymn is a revelation, though it was given unto us by a woman—Sister Eliza R. Snow. There are a great many sisters who have the spirit of revelation. There is no reason why they should not be inspired as well as men.[7]

We cannot find anywhere within the lids of the Bible where the Lord ever had a people he acknowledged, except they were led by immediate revelation.[8]

If this people would rise up and do their duty, when men rise before them in this stand to point out the way of life, the Spirit of the Lord would reveal the things necessary for the people to understand, for the faith of the people would draw them out. All that is required is for the people to arouse themselves, and get the light of God within them.[9]

HE LIVED AS HE TAUGHT

REMARKABLE CONVERSIONS AT BENBOW FARM

Late in 1839, thirty-two-year-old Wilford Woodruff—who had been ordained an apostle earlier that year—was called on a mission to Great Britain. Because of his willingness to follow the Spirit, Elder Woodruff was blessed to participate in one of the great missionary experiences of this dispensation. In his own words:

"March 1st, 1840, was my birthday; I was thirty-three years of age. It being Sunday, I preached twice during the day to a large assembly in the city hall, in the town of Hanley, and administered the Sacrament to the Saints. In the evening I again met with a large assembly of the Saints and strangers, and while singing the first hymn the spirit of the Lord rested upon me and the voice of God said to me, 'This is the last meeting that you will hold with this people for many days.' I was astonished at this, as I had many appointments out in that district. When I arose to speak to the people, I told them that it was the last meeting I should hold with them for many days. They were as much astonished as I was. At the close of the meeting four persons came forward for baptism; we went down into the water and baptized them.

"In the morning I went in secret before the Lord, and asked Him what was His will concerning me. The answer I received was that I should go to the south; for the Lord had a great work for me to perform there, as many souls were waiting for His word. On the 3rd of March, 1840, in fulfillment of the directions given me, I took coach and rode to Wolverhampton, twenty-six miles, spending the night there. On the morning of the 4th I again took coach, and rode through Dudley, Stourbridge, Stourport, and Worcester, then walked a number of miles to Mr. John Benbow's, Hill Farm, Castle Frome, Ledbury, Herefordshire. This was a farming country in the south of England, a region where no elder of the Latter-day Saints had visited.

"I found Mr. Benbow to be a wealthy farmer, cultivating three hundred acres of land, occupying a good mansion, and having plenty of means. His wife, Jane, had no children. I presented myself to him as a missionary from America, an elder of the Church of Jesus Christ of Latter-day Saints, who had been sent to him by the commandment of God as a messenger of salvation, to preach the gospel of life to him and his household and the inhabitants of the land. He and his wife received me with glad hearts and thanksgiving. It was in the evening when I arrived, having traveled forty-eight miles by coach and on foot during the day, but after receiving refreshments we sat down together, and conversed until two o'clock in the morning. Mr. Benbow and his wife rejoiced greatly at the glad tidings which I brought them.

"I also rejoiced greatly at the news Mr. Benbow gave me, that there was a company of men and women—over six hundred in number—who had broken off from the Wesleyan Methodists, and taken the name of United Brethren. They had forty-five preachers among them, and for religious services had chapels and many houses that were licensed according to the law of the land. This body of United Brethren were searching for light and truth, but had gone as far as they could, and were calling upon the Lord continually to open the way before them and send them light and knowledge, that they might know the true way to be saved. When I heard these things I could clearly see why the Lord had commanded me, while in the town of Hanley, to leave that place of labor and go to the south; for in Herefordshire there was a great harvest-field for gathering many saints into the Kingdom of God. After offering my prayers and thanksgiving to God, I retired to my bed with joy, and slept well until the rising of the sun.

"I arose on the morning of the 5th, took breakfast, and told Mr. Benbow I would like to commence my Master's business by preaching the gospel to the people. He had in his mansion a large hall which was licensed for preaching, and he sent word through the neighborhood that an American missionary would preach at his house that evening. As the time drew nigh, many of the neighbors came in, and I preached my first gospel sermon in the house. I also preached at the same place on the following evening, and baptized six persons, including Mr. John Benbow, his wife, and four preachers of the United Brethren. I spent most of the following day in clearing out a pool of water and preparing it for baptizing, as I saw that many would receive that ordinance. I afterwards baptized six hundred persons in that pool of water.

"On Sunday, the 8th, I preached at Frome's Hill in the morning, at Standley Hill in the afternoon, and at John Benbow's, Hill Farm, in the evening. The parish church that stood in the neighborhood of Brother Benbow's, presided over by the rector of the parish, was attended during the day by only fifteen persons, while I had a large congregation, estimated to number a thousand, attend my meetings through the day and evening.

"When I arose to speak at Brother Benbow's house, a man entered the door and informed me that he was a constable, and had been sent by the rector of the parish with a warrant to arrest me. I asked him, 'For what crime?' He said, 'For preaching to the people.' I told him that I, as well as the rector, had a license for preaching the gospel to the people, and that if he would take a chair I would wait upon him after meeting. He took my chair and sat beside me. For an hour and a quarter I preached the first principles of the everlasting gospel. The power of God rested upon me, the spirit filled the house, and the people were convinced. At the close of the meeting I opened the door for baptism, and seven offered themselves. Among the number were four preachers and the constable. The latter arose and said, 'Mr. Woodruff, I would like to be baptized.' I told him I would like to baptize him. I went down into the pool and baptized the seven. We then came together. I confirmed thirteen, administered the Sacrament, and we all rejoiced together.

"The constable went to the rector and told him that if he wanted Mr. Woodruff taken for preaching the gospel, he must go himself and serve the writ; for he had heard him preach the only true gospel sermon he had ever listened to in his life. The rector did not know what to make of it, so he sent two clerks of the Church of England as spies, to attend our meeting, and find out what we did preach. They both were pricked in their hearts, received the word of the Lord gladly, and were baptized and confirmed members of the Church of Jesus Christ of Latter-day Saints. The rector became alarmed, and did not venture to send anybody else.

"The ministers and rectors of the south of England called a convention and sent a petition to the Archbishop of Canterbury, to request Parliament to pass a law prohibiting the Mormons from preaching in the British dominions. In this petition the rectors stated that one Mormon missionary had baptized fifteen hundred persons, mostly members of the English Church, during the past seven months. But the Archbishop and council, knowing well that the laws of England afforded toleration to all religions under the British flag, sent word to the petitioners that if they had the worth of souls at heart as much as they valued ground where hares, foxes, and hounds ran, they would not lose so many of their flock.

"I continued to preach and baptize daily. On the 21st day of March I baptized Elder Thomas Kington. He was superintendent of both preachers and members of the United Brethren. The first thirty days after my arrival in Herefordshire, I had baptized forty-five preachers and one hundred and sixty members of the United Brethren, who put into my hands one chapel and forty-five houses, which were licensed according to law to preach in. This opened a wide field for labor, and enabled me to bring into the Church, through the blessings of God, over eighteen hundred souls during eight months, including all of the six hundred United Brethren except one person. In this number there were also some two hundred preachers of various denominations. This field of labor embraced Herefordshire, Gloucestershire, and Worcestershire, and formed the conferences of Garway, Gadfield Elm, and Frome's Hill."[10]

"That Warning of the Spirit Rested upon Me"

In 1891, eighty-four-year-old Wilford Woodruff stood to deliver an address in the Tabernacle. Ordained President of the Church two years earlier, he had served as an apostle for fifty-two years. He had served missions to Kentucky, Canada, New England, and Great Britain (twice). A prolific journal keeper, he recorded seven thousand pages of diaries between 1833 and 1898. In the address excerpted below, as in many others, President Woodruff spoke on one of his favorite themes—following the Spirit:

"I will now tell you one incident where I did not obey the Spirit of the Lord, and it came pretty near costing me my life. I was over at Randolph one December, visiting. On Monday morning the Spirit said to me, 'Take your team and go home.' I made up my mind to do it; but some of my friends felt anxious that I should stop, as my visit had been rather short, and I was persuaded to stop. I stayed until Saturday morning, but I felt uneasy. That warning of the Spirit rested upon me to that degree that I felt condemned, and I told my friends that I was going home. I ate an early breakfast that morning, put my horses to my wagon, took some hay and grain, and started for home by way of Wasatch, which was some thirty miles from there. When I got to Woodruff, the bishop wanted me to stay and hold a meeting there on Sunday.

"'No,' says I, 'I have already stayed too long by one week.'

"Well, after I got about three miles from Woodruff, which is fifteen miles from Wasatch, I met with one of the most terrific snowstorms I ever saw in my life. Five minutes after it commenced I could not see the road. I could not guide my horses at all, so I let them go where they pleased. They had been twice over the ground before. I shut down the wagon cover and went to praying. I asked the Lord to forgive me for not obeying his commandments. At eight o'clock my horses carried me into Wasatch, the hubs of the wheels

28

being under the snow. I think they must have got there by inspiration. I stayed there until Monday night. I made up my mind then that whenever the Lord told me to do anything I would do it."[11]

Wilford Woodruff was born 1 March 1807 in Farmington, Connecticut, to Aphek Woodruff and Beulah Thompson. Married Phoebe Carter 13 April 1837. Five wives, thirty-three children. Ordained an apostle 26 April 1839 at age thirty-two by Brigham Young. Sustained as President of the Church 7 April 1889 at age eighty-two. Died 2 September 1898 in San Francisco, California, at age ninety-two.

5

"TRIALS WILL PROVE
BLESSINGS IN DISGUISE"

THE WORDS HE LIVED BY

Born in 1814, Lorenzo Snow grew up in comfortable circumstances in Ohio. He joined the Church in 1836, after his older sister Eliza, who had previously been baptized, arranged for him to meet the Prophet Joseph Smith. Within months Lorenzo began traveling throughout his home state of Ohio, preaching the gospel without purse or scrip. Over his long missionary career he preached the gospel in Kentucky, Missouri, and the surrounding states; Great Britain (where he presented Queen Victoria with a copy of the Book of Mormon); Italy (where he supervised the translation of the Book of Mormon into Italian), Switzerland, Malta, and Gibraltar; Hawaii; and what was then the northwestern United States, where he labored among the Lamanites. From illness to accidents to the passing of loved ones, Lorenzo Snow overcame continual trials in his life. In his sermons, he frequently admonished the Saints to endure trials with faith:

> Brethren and sisters, I was delighted in listening to the first hymn sung by the choir today in these services. To me the words are full of significance and promise. They are verily true and were indited by the spirit of truth. . . .
>
> *Every human tie may perish,*
> *Friend to friend unfaithful prove,*
> *Mothers cease their own to cherish,*
> *Heaven and earth at last remove;*
> *But no changes*
> *Can attend Jehovah's love.*
>
> *In the furnace God may prove thee,*
> *Thence to bring thee forth more bright,*
> *But can never cease to love thee—*
> *Thou art precious in his sight;*
> *God is with thee;*
> *Thou shalt triumph in his might.*

This is very encouraging to the Latter-day Saints. It gives the assurance that the love of God can never change towards them. They may be afflicted and pass through numerous trials of a severe character, but these will prove blessings in disguise and bring them out brighter and better than they were before. The people of God are precious in His sight; His love for them will always endure, and in His might and strength and affection, they will triumph and be brought off more than conqueror. . . .

There is no necessity for Latter-day Saints to worry over the things of this world. They will all pass away. Our hearts should be set on things above; to strive after that perfection which was in Christ Jesus, who was perfectly obedient in all things unto the Father, and so obtained His great exaltation and became a pattern unto His brethren. Why should we fret and worry over these temporal things when our destiny is so grand and glorious? If we will cleave unto the Lord, keep His commandments, pattern after His perfections and reach out unto the eternal realities of His heavenly kingdom, all will be well with us and we shall triumph and obtain the victory in the end.[1]

President Snow taught that our trials and adversities are given for a purpose. They school us, giving us necessary experience and helping us to prepare for things to come.

The trials and temptations have been very great to many of our people and more or less, perhaps, to all of us. The Lord seems to require some proof on our part, something to show that He can depend upon us when He wants us to accomplish certain things in His interest. The reason is that . . . in the future, as time passes along, as eternity approaches, and as we move forward in eternity and along the line of our existence, we shall be placed in certain conditions that require very great sacrifice in the interests of humanity, in the interests of the Spirit of God, in the interest of His children and our own children, in generations to come, in eternity.[2]

We are here that we may be educated in a school of suffering and of fiery trials, which school was necessary for Jesus our Elder Brother, who, the Scriptures tell us, was made perfect through suffering. It is necessary we suffer in all things, that we may be qualified and worthy to rule and govern all things, even as our Father in heaven and His Eldest Son Jesus.[3]

HE LIVED AS HE TAUGHT

THE FURNACE OF AFFLICTION

Lorenzo's determination to overcome trials enabled him to receive unique revelations and do a great work among the Saints. Some of those trials included the following:

• Enduring a serious illness not long after he was baptized. During a journey from Kirtland, Ohio, to Missouri, "Lorenzo became very ill with a fever, which caused terrific head pains. So severe were the pains that his sister, Eliza, cradled his head in her lap to cushion it from the rocking and lurching of the wagon."[4]

• Leaving on a mission while still recovering from these health problems. He met with little success, sometimes fearing for his life because of mobs. Then, "the 500-mile walk home in the rough winter weather took its toll on him. When he reached his destination, he was initially denied entrance to the home of a relative because he was so haggard and emaciated. After a bout of violent fever and delirium, he finally recovered."[5]

• Enduring another serious illness in 1847 at Pisgah, Iowa. "At this place," he wrote, "I was taken seriously and dangerously ill with a burning fever, which so affected my brain that I was delirious many days, lying at the point of death. While in this condition, [some of the brethren] took me from my bed, wrapped in a sheet—placed me in a carriage, drove to a stream of water, and baptized me in the name of the Lord, for my recovery. The fever immediately abated, and through kind, unwearied nursing and attention by my faithful, loving wives, and my dear sister [Eliza] . . . I was delivered from suffering and restored to health."[6]

• Losing his wife Charlotte while he was serving a mission to Europe. She died on 25 September 1850. When Elder Snow finally returned to Utah in 1852, he wrote: "Arriving at my home in Salt Lake City, the long anticipated oasis of this portion of my life-journey, the beacon light which succeeded my arduous missionary labors, and shone with a brighter beam than all other earthly luminaries, the happiness of once again meeting my loved and loving family would have been full, but alas! there was a sad vacancy. A lovely one was not; one who ever met me with a smiling face and a loving heart, was not there to respond to love's sacred call; Charlotte, my dear wife, had been stricken down by death, and her beautiful form lay mouldering in the silent tomb. Yet there was consolation in the thought that her pure spirit was mingling with holy beings above. A short time after Charlotte's decease, while I was in Italy, a sister in London, a very faithful Saint, the wife of Elder Jabez Woodard, had an open vision, in which she saw a beautiful woman, the most lovely being she ever beheld, clothed in white robes and crowned with glory. This personage told Mrs. Woodard that she was a wife of Lorenzo Snow."[7]

• Almost drowning when a boat capsized in Hawaii. His missionary companions had almost given him up for dead when he was miraculously revived by the power of the priesthood.[8]

• Being imprisoned for practicing plural marriage. He was held for nine months in the Utah Territorial Prison in 1886, when he was seventy-two years old.[9]

LORENZO SNOW'S VISION OF THE SAVIOR

Lorenzo Snow endured one of his final trials after being called as President of the Church. Describing this trial—and the wonderful blessing that followed—his son Leroi wrote:

"For some time President Woodruff's health had been failing. Nearly every evening President Lorenzo Snow visited him at his home. . . . This particular evening the doctors said President Woodruff was failing rapidly and they feared he would not live much longer.

"Lorenzo Snow was then President of the Council of Twelve and was greatly worried over the possibility of suceeding President Woodruff, especially because of the terrible financial condition of the Church. Referring to this condition, President Heber J. Grant has said: 'The Church was in a financial slough of despond, so to speak, almost financially bankrupt—its credit was hardly good for a thousand dollars without security.'

"My father went to his room in the Salt Lake Temple, where he was residing at the time. He dressed in his robes of the Priesthood, went into the Holy of Holies, there in the House of the Lord and knelt at the sacred altar. He pled with the Lord to spare President Woodruff's life, that President Woodruff might outlive him and that the great responsibility of Church leadership would never fall upon his shoulders. Yet he promised the Lord that he would devotedly perform any duty required at his hands. At this time he was in his eighty-sixth year.

"Soon after this President Woodruff was taken to California where he died Friday morning at 6:40 o'clock, September 2, 1898. President George Q. Cannon at once wired the information to the President's office in Salt Lake City. Word was forwarded to President Snow, who was in Brigham City. The telegram was delivered to him on the street in Brigham. He read it to President

Rudger Clawson, then president of Box Elder Stake, who was with him, went to the telegraph office and replied that he would leave on the train about 5:30 that evening. He reached Salt Lake City about 7:15, proceeded to the President's office, gave some instructions and then went to his private room in the Salt Lake Temple.

"President Snow put on his holy temple robes, repaired again to the same sacred altar, offered up the signs of the Priesthood, and poured out his heart to the Lord. He reminded the Lord how he pled for President Woodruff's life. . . . 'Nevertheless,' he said, 'Thy will be done. I have not sought this responsibility but if it be Thy will, I now present myself before Thee for Thy guidance and instruction. I ask that Thou show me what Thou wouldst have me do.'

"After finishing his prayer he expected a reply, some special manifestation from the Lord. So he waited—and waited—and waited. There was no reply, no voice, no visitation, no manifestation. He left the altar and the room in great disappointment. He passed through the Celestial room and out into the large corridor, where a most glorious manifestation was given President Snow. . . ."[10]

At this point the narrative proceeds with the words of a granddaughter of President Snow, Allie Young Pond:

"One evening while I was visiting grandpa Snow in his room in the Salt Lake Temple, I remained until the door keepers had gone and the nightwatchman had not yet come in, so Grandpa said he would take me to the main front entrance and let me out that way. He got his bunch of keys from his dresser.

"After we left his room and while we were still in the large corridor leading into the Celestial room, I was walking several steps ahead of Grandpa when he stopped me, saying: 'Wait a moment, Allie, I want to tell you something. It was right here that the Lord Jesus Christ appeared to me at the time of the death of President

36

Woodruff. He instructed me to go right ahead and reorganize the First Presidency of the Church at once and not wait as had been done after the death of the previous presidents, and that I was to succeed President Woodruff.'

"Then Grandpa came a step nearer and held out his left hand and said: 'He stood right here, about three feet above the floor. It looked as though He stood on a plate of solid gold.'

"Grandpa told me what a glorious personage the Savior is and described His hands, feet, countenance and beautiful white robes, all of which were of such a glory of whiteness and brightness that he could hardly gaze upon Him.

"Then Grandpa came another step nearer me and put his right hand on my head and said: 'Now, granddaughter, I want you to remember that this is the testimony of your grandfather, that he told you with his own lips that he actually saw the Savior, here in the Temple, and talked with Him face to face.'"[11]

This experience, and many others, underscored and reinforced the teaching that was a theme to President Snow: The Saints "may be afflicted and pass through numerous trials of a severe character, but these will prove blessings in disguise and bring them out brighter and better than they were before."[12]

Lorenzo Snow was born 3 April 1814 in Mantua, Ohio, to Oliver Snow and Rosetta Pettibone. Married Charlotte Squires and Mary Adaline Goddard (in the same ceremony in the Nauvoo Temple) in January of 1846. Nine wives, forty-two children. Ordained an apostle 12 February 1849 at age thirty-four by Heber C. Kimball. Ordained President of the Church 13 September 1898 at age eighty-four. Died 10 October 1901 in Salt Lake City at age eighty-seven.

6

"PROVE TO YOUR CHILDREN THAT YOU LOVE THEM BY YOUR EVERY WORD AND ACT"

Joseph F. Smith

THE WORDS HE LIVED BY

Reminiscing about his father, Joseph F. Smith, Joseph Fielding Smith wrote: "His love for his wives and children was boundless in its magnitude and purity. The world did not know—could not possibly know—the depths of his love for them. The wicked and the depraved have ridiculed and maligned him; but the true condition of his family life and wonderful love for his family is beyond their comprehension. O how he prayed that his children would always be *true*—true to God, true to their fellow men; true to each other and true to him! 'The richest of all my earthly joys is in my precious children,' he was wont to say. In return the children should say the richest of all their earthly joys are found in having such a father. Let them, one and all, be true to him and true to the cause which he represented so faithfully for the period of his mortal life, and which was the dearest thing to him in all his life."[1]

Joseph F. Smith taught these principles fervently:

> Brethren, . . . if you will keep your [children] close to your heart, within the clasp of your arms; if you will make them . . . feel that you love them . . . and keep them near to you, they will not go very far from you, and they will not commit any very great sin. But it is when you turn them out of the home, turn them out of your affection . . . that [is what] drives them from you. . . .
>
> Fathers, if you wish your children to be taught in the principles of the gospel, if you wish them to love the truth and understand it, if you wish them to be obedient to and united with you, love them! and prove . . . that you do love them by your every word and act to[ward] them.[2]

Men and women understand the importance of taking care of business affairs, President Smith taught. Isn't it as least as important to attend to the needs of their children?

> Are we studying their wants as we do our business, and our farms and our animals? Are we looking after them, and if necessary bringing them in from the street when absent, and providing them in our homes with what they lack? Or are we to a great extent neglecting these things in the home and home training, and considering our children of secondary value to horses and cattle and lands?[3]

Both in his life and in his teachings, President Smith showed that unfeigned love was the key:

> For your own sake, for the love that should exist between you and your boys, however wayward they might be, . . . when you

39

speak or talk to them, do it not in anger, do it not harshly, in a condemning spirit. Speak to them kindly; get them down and weep with them if necessary and get them to shed tears with you if possible. Soften their hearts; get them to feel tenderly toward you. Use no lash and no violence, but argue, or rather reason— approach them with reason, with persuasion and love unfeigned.

Such love and tenderness are the only means a parent can truly reach a child:

> With these means, if you cannot gain your boys and your girls, they will prove to be reprobate to you; and there will be no means left in the world by which you can win them to yourselves. But, get them to feel as you feel, have interest in the things in which you take interest, to love the gospel as you love it, to love one another as you love them; to love their parents as the parents love the children. You can't do it any other way. You can't do it by unkindness; you cannot do it by driving; our children are like we are; we couldn't be driven; we can't be driven now. We are like some other animals that we know of in the world. You can coax them; you can lead them, by holding out inducements to them, and by speaking kindly to them, but you can't drive them; they won't be driven. We won't be driven. Men are not in the habit of being driven; they are not made that way.

This is not the way that God intended, in the beginning, to deal with his children—by force. It is all free love, free grace. The poet expressed it in these words:

> "Know this, that every soul is free,
> To choose his life and what he'll be;
> For this eternal truth is given,
> That God will force no man to heaven."

You can't force your boys, nor your girls into heaven. You may force them to hell, by using harsh means in the efforts to make them good, when you yourselves are not as good as you should be. The man that will be angry at his boy, and try to correct him while he is in anger, is in the greatest fault; he is more to be pitied and more to be condemned than the child who has done wrong. You can only correct your children by love, in kindness, by love unfeigned, by persuasion, and reason.[4]

HE LIVED AS HE TAUGHT

"No Love Can Equal the Love of a True Mother"

Joseph F. Smith lost his father, Hyrum, when he was five years old. As the following tributes show, he learned much about the power of love from his mother, Mary Fielding Smith:

"When I was a child, somewhat a wayward, disobedient little boy—not that I was wilfully disobedient, but I would forget what I ought to do; I would go off with playful boys and be absent when I should have been at home, and I would forget to do things I was asked to do. Then I would go home, feel guilty, know that I was guilty, that I had neglected my duty and that I deserved punishment.

"On one occasion I had done something that was not just right, and my mother said to me: 'Now, Joseph, if you do that again I shall have to whip you.' Well, time went on, and by and by, I forgot it, and I did something similar again; and this is the one thing that I admired more, perhaps, than any secondary thing in her; it was that when she made a promise she kept it. She never made a promise, that I know of, that she did not keep.

"Well, I was called to account. She said: 'Now, I told you. You knew that if you did this I would have to whip you, for I said I would. I must do it. I do not want to do it. It hurts me worse than it does you, but I must whip you.'

"Well, she had a little rawhide, already there, and while she was talking or reasoning with me, showing me how much I deserved it and how painful it was to her, to inflict the punishment I deserved, I had only one thought and that was: 'For goodness' sake whip me; do not reason with me,' for I felt the lash of her just criticism and admonition a thousand fold worse than I did the switch. I felt as if, when she laid the lash on me, I had at least partly paid my debt and had answered for my wrong doing. Her reasoning cut me down into the quick; it made me feel sorry to the very core!

"I could have endured a hundred lashes with the rawhide better than I could endure a ten-minutes' talk in which I felt and was made to feel that the punishment inflicted upon me was painful to her that I loved—punishment upon my own mother!"[5]

"I learned in my childhood, as most children, probably, have learned, more or less at least, that no love in all the world can equal the love of a true mother.

"I did not think in those days, and still I am at a loss to know, how it would be possible for anyone to love her children more truly than did my mother. I have felt sometimes, how could even the Father love his children more than my mother loved her children? It was life to me; it was strength; it was encouragement; it was love that begat love or liking in myself. I knew she loved me with all her heart. She loved her children with all her soul. She would toil and labor and sacrifice herself day and night, for the temporal comforts and blessings that she could meagerly give, through the results of her own labors, to her children. There was no sacrifice of self—of her own time, of her leisure or pleasure, or opportunities for rest—

that was considered for a moment, when it was compared with her duty and her love to her children.

"When I was fifteen years of age, and called to go to a foreign country to preach the gospel—or to learn how, and to learn it for myself—the strongest anchor that was fixed in my life, and that helped to hold my ambition and my desire steady, to bring me upon a level and keep me straight, was that love which I knew she had for me who bore me into the world.

"Only a little boy, not matured at all in judgment, without the advantage of education, thrown in the midst of the greatest allurements and temptations that it was possible for any boy or any man to be subjected to—and yet, whenever these temptations became most alluring and most tempting to me, the first thought that arose in my soul was this: Remember the love of your mother. Remember how she strove for your welfare. Remember how willing she was to sacrifice her life for your good. Remember what she taught you in your childhood and how she insisted upon your reading the New Testament—the only book, except a few little school books, that we had in the family, or that was within reach of us at that time. This feeling toward my mother became a defense, a barrier between me and temptation, so that I could turn aside from temptation and sin by the help of the Lord and the love begotten in my soul, toward her whom I knew loved me more than anybody else in all the world, and more than any other living being could love me.

"A wife may love her husband, but it is different to that of the love of mother to her child. The true mother, the mother who has the fear of God and the love of truth in her soul, would never hide from danger or evil and leave her child exposed to it. But as natural as it is for the sparks to fly upward, as natural as it is to breathe the breath of life, if there were danger coming to her child, she would step between the child and that danger; she would defend her child to the uttermost. Her life would be nothing in the balance, in comparison with the life of her child. That is the love of true motherhood for children.

"Her love for her husband would be different, for if danger should come to him, as natural as it would be for her to step between her child and danger, instead, her disposition would be to step behind her husband for protection, and that is the difference between the love of mother for children and the love of wife for husband—there is a great difference between the two.

"I have learned to place a high estimate upon the love of mother. I have often said, and will repeat it, that the love of a true mother comes nearer being like the love of God than any other kind of love."[6]

"She Took Me in and Was a Mother to Me"

Sadly, the already fatherless Joseph F. Smith lost his mother, Mary Fielding Smith, when he was only thirteen—and his sister Martha Ann eleven. Mary died on 21 September 1852 in Salt Lake City; she was fifty-one years old. "After my mother's death," he later wrote, "there followed 18 months—from Sept 21st, 1852 to April, 1854 of perilous times for me. I was almost like a comet or fiery meteor, without attraction or gravitation to keep me balanced or guide me within reasonable bounds."[7]

Called on a mission to Hawaii at age fifteen, Joseph F. suffered loneliness and a severe illness, possibly yellow fever. A Hawaiian woman named Ma Mahuhii become a surrogate mother to him, nursing him back to health and offering a stability that helped him recover from the loss of his parents. Many years later, when President Smith and Bishop Charles W. Nibley visited the islands, Joseph F. was reunited with his second mother. Bishop Nibley recalled:

"I noticed a poor, old blind woman tottering under the weight

44

of about ninety years, being led [into the meetinghouse where the Saints were gathering to greet President Joseph F.]. She had a few choice bananas in her hand. It was her all—her offering. She was calling 'Iosepa, Iosepa!' Instantly, when he saw her, he ran to her and clasped her in his arms, hugged her, and kissed her over and over again, patting her on the head saying, 'Mama, Mama, my dear old Mama!'

"And with tears streaming down his cheeks he turned to me and said, 'Charley, she nursed me when I was a boy, sick and without anyone to care for me. She took me in and was a mother to me!'"[8]

LETTERS TO HIS DAUGHTER

The love he felt from both his mother and his second mother had a powerful effect on Joseph F. Smith, who became passionately devoted to his own children. His letter writing to his daughter Emily typified the love and concern he felt for all of his children. When Emily, then in her twenties, took a trip to the East, President Smith wrote frequent letters, one day sending two of them. At virtually every stop she made along the way, Emily found a letter waiting from her "dear Papa."

When President Smith traveled to Hawaii in May of 1915 to dedicate the site of the future temple, he offered a powerful prayer. "Never in all my life," recalled Elder Reed Smoot, "did I hear such a prayer. The very ground seemed to be sacred, and he seemed as if he were talking face to face with the Father. I cannot and never will forget it if I live a thousand years."[9]

But even in the midst of preparing for such an important event, President Smith had been focusing on his children. On his arrival in Honolulu, he sent a "Passenger List Souvenir" card addressed to "My Darling Emily and Edith. Beehive House." Decorated with a colorful scene of a ship steaming toward the setting sun, the card also included a map of the Pacific and a "Steamship Log," where President Smith had noted the miles traveled each day: May 16—296; May 17—330; May 18—340; May 19—351; May 20—351; May 21—355. "We arrived in the harbor at Honolulu about 5 P.M.," he wrote, "and were detained by the quarantine physicians an hour and a half. When we landed we went to the mission house and then to bro. and sister Fernandez for the night, and came here to Laie Saturday 22d."[10]

"My Precious, Darling Emily," President Smith wrote in March of 1918, eight months before his death, "Thank you for your interesting letter of the 4th which came on the 6th and found us all usually well but 'enjoying' a protracted, continuous, copious, soaking rain Storme. . . . No parents ever had better, Sweeter, more loveable, truer children than your Sweet mother and me! unworthy as I may be. . . . Now my beloved, true, faithful devoted Emily, There is nothing too good for *you*. And while I have anything you are more than welcome to your full share of it and you shall have it without the asking, but if I should fail to see what you need, it is your privilege and your right to say to me—papa—*I need!* And you shall have!

"God bless you, my precious daughter and make your life full of happiness and joy. . . . Ever affectionately Your Papa."[11]

Joseph F. Smith was born 13 November 1838 in Far West, Missouri, to Hyrum Smith and Mary Fielding. Married Levira Smith 4 April 1859. Six wives, forty-eight children. Ordained an apostle 1 July 1866 at age twenty-seven by Brigham Young. Ordained President of the Church 17 October 1901 at age sixty-two. Died 19 November 1918 in Salt Lake City at age eighty.

7

"THE GOSPEL ROBS THE GRAVE OF ITS STING"

Heber J. Grant

THE WORDS HE LIVED BY

Heber J. Grant was a man of many convictions. Though he preached a variety of public sermons on such topics as the Word of Wisdom, missionary work, temple ordinances, and staying out of debt, President Grant also testified of the truthfulness of the gospel in quiet, personal ways. This was particularly true in regard to the comfort the gospel offers to those who have lost loved ones. Both in his personal losses and in his comfort to others, Heber J. Grant continually demonstrated that the atonement and resurrection of the Savior provide lasting, genuine consolation for the bereaved.

The following statements typify President Grant's attitude:

Death seems a most terrible thing, as near as I can judge by attending the funerals of people where the surviving relatives do not know the truth, but to a Latter-day Saint, while death brings sorrow into our homes and our hearts, that sorrow is more or less of the same nature that we feel when we are temporarily called upon to part with our dear ones who are going out into the mission field or who are moving away for some time. That awful anguish that I have seen exhibited by those who know not the truth, I believe never comes into the heart of a true Latter-day Saint.

It has fallen to my lot to part with two wives, to part with a beloved mother, to bury both of my sons, one daughter, and most of my life-long friends, and yet I do not believe that I have suffered at all in comparison to what I have seen others suffer who know not the truth.[1]

I regret ofttimes, in the times of distress and trouble that come to those whom we admire and love, that we are not able to lift from their shoulders the sorrow into which they are plunged, when they are called upon to part with those they cherish.

But we realize that our Father in heaven can bind up broken hearts and that He can dispel sorrow and that He can point forward with joy and satisfaction to those blessings that are to come through obedience to the Gospel of the Lord Jesus Christ, for we do understand and we do have conviction that it is the will of our Father in heaven that we shall live on and that we have not finished our existence when these bodies of mortality are laid away in the grave.

It is a very great blessing that in the providences of the Lord and in the revelations that have been given by our Father in heaven, we have the assurance that the spirit and the body, in due time, will be reunited, notwithstanding the unbelief that there is in the world today—and there certainly is great skepticism and unbelief in relation to this matter. But notwithstanding this, we have assurance through the revelations that have been given by the Lord our God, that that is the purpose of God, that the body and the spirit shall be eternally united and that there will come a time, through the blessing and mercy of God, when we will no more have sorrow but when we shall have conquered all of these things that are of a trying and distressing character, and shall stand up in the presence of the living God, filled with joy and peace and satisfaction.[2]

HE LIVED AS HE TAUGHT

"I CAN ONLY ASK OUR HEAVENLY FATHER TO WATCH AND GUARD YOU"

Early in his life, Heber began writing heartfelt letters of condolence to those who had lost loved ones. In 1880, for example, two years before he was ordained an apostle, twenty-three-year-old Heber wrote such a letter to his cousin and good friend Anthony W. Ivins and his wife, Elizabeth, who had just lost their three-month-old boy, Anthony. (The elder Anthony was ordained an apostle in 1907 and later served in the First Presidency with President Grant.) "My Dear Cousins Tony and Libbie," wrote Heber, "It was with sorrow that I learned of the death of your little darling. If I could say or do anything that would in the least lessen your sorrow, God knows that I would most willingly do so. I can only ask our Heavenly Father, He who gives and takes away to comfort you in this your hour of need, and to ask Him to watch and guard you through this life that you may be prepared to meet your darling in His Kingdom. The poet says: 'These are more sad than happy hours[.]' We all know the truth of these few words, and in our sorrows and afflictions it is hard to acknowledge the hand of God, still we know that he does all things well. Your little one is safe from the cares, sorrows and temptations of this world . . . knowing as we do that if we are faithful our separation at the most will be but a short one.

Once more asking God to comfort your aching hearts I remain with feelings of sympathy and esteem[,] Your Cousin Heber."[3]

THE LOSS OF A SON

Heber J. Grant took great joy in his ten daughters, most of whom lived long lives. One of the trials of his life, however, was losing both of his sons when they were young. Daniel Wells died in March 1895, and Heber Stringham died less than a year later, in February 1896. Still, Heber met these hardships with the same faith he encouraged others to have. Concerning young Heber's death, he later wrote:

"I have been blessed with only two sons. One of them died at five years of age and the other at seven.

"My last son died of a hip disease. I had built great hopes that he would live to spread the gospel at home and abroad and be an honor to me. About an hour before he died I had a dream that his mother, who was dead, came for him, and that she brought with her a messenger, and she told this messenger to take the boy while I was asleep. In the dream I thought I awoke and I seized my son and fought for him and finally succeeded in getting him away from the messenger who had come to take him, and in so doing I dreamed that I stumbled and fell upon him.

"I dreamed that I fell upon his sore hip, and the terrible cries and anguish of the child drove me nearly wild. I could not stand it, and I jumped up and ran out of the house so as not to hear his distress. I dreamed that after running out of the house I met Brother Joseph E. Taylor and told him of these things.

"He said: 'Well, Heber, do you know what I would do if my wife came for one of her children—I would not struggle for that child; I would not oppose her taking that child away. If a mother who had been faithful had passed beyond the veil, she would know of the suffering and the anguish her child may have to suffer. She would know whether that child might go through life as a cripple and whether it would be better or wiser for that child to be relieved from the torture of life. And when you stop to think, Brother Grant, that the mother of that boy went down into the shadow of death to give him life, she is the one who ought to have the right to take him or leave him.'

"I said, 'I believe you are right, Brother Taylor, and if she comes again, she shall have the boy without any protest on my part.'

"After coming to that conclusion, I was waked by my brother, B. F. Grant, who was staying that night with us.

"He called me into the room and told me that my child was dying.

"I went in the front room and sat down. There was a vacant chair between me and my wife who is now living, and I felt the presence of that boy's deceased mother, sitting in that chair. I did not tell anybody what I felt, but I turned to my living wife and said: 'Do you feel anything strange?' She said: 'Yes, I feel assured that Heber's mother is sitting between us, waiting to take him away.'

"Now, I am naturally, I believe, a sympathetic man. I was raised as an only child with all the affection that a mother could lavish upon a boy. I believe that I am naturally affectionate and sympathetic and that I shed tears for my friends—tears of joy for their success and tears of sorrow for their misfortunes. But I sat by the deathbed of my little boy and saw him die, without shedding a tear. My living wife, my brother, and I, upon that occasion experienced a sweet, peaceful, and heavenly influence in my home, as great as I have ever experienced in my life. And no person can tell me that every other Latter-day Saint that has a knowledge of the gospel in his heart and soul, can really mourn for his loved ones; only in the loss of their society here in this life.

"I never think of my wives and my dear mother and my two boys, my daughter, and my departed friends, and beloved associates being in the graveyard. I think only of the joy and the happiness and the peace and satisfaction that my mother is having in meeting with the Prophet and the Patriarch and Brigham Young and my father and the beloved friends that she knew from the days of Nauvoo to the day that she died. I think only of the joy they have in meeting with father and mother and loved ones who have been true and faithful to the gospel of the Lord Jesus Christ. My mind reaches out to the wonderful joy and satisfaction and happiness that they are having, and it robs the grave of its sting."[4]

"HIS REMEMBRANCE CARRIED HER THROUGH THE ORDEAL"

Along with sending letters, President Grant also sent books as a permanent remembrance of those who had died. He signed them, often underlining some of his favorite passages. Over the years he sent thousands of books. His daughter Lucy recalled:

"For forty-one years it was my privilege to visit the various stakes of Zion. I think I can truthfully say that seldom did I go to any outlying stake that some one of the congregation did not tell me of Father's gifts. He helped widows, missionaries, people who had lost their loved ones, those who had been in accidents, or those whose people had been killed or injured in an accident. While I was in Wyoming, one woman who husband had been killed in a mine accident came to me and she told me that Father had written her a personal letter. He sent books to her, and to her children, about eight in number, and she told how that letter and those books, and his remembrance carried her through the ordeal which she otherwise could not have endured."[5]

THE PASSING OF ANTHONY W. IVINS

In September of 1934, fifty-four years after Heber had sent a letter to Tony and Libby Ivins concerning the death of their baby boy,

President Ivins passed away at the age of eighty-two. Close friends throughout their lives, he and Heber had served together in the Quorum of the Twelve for eleven years and in the First Presidency for thirteen years. Once again, President Grant's faith in Christ and love for others shone through:

"My dear Libbie . . . ," wrote President Grant, "Gusta [Heber's wife, Augusta Winters Grant] joins me in sending our heartfelt sympathy to you on account of the death of your beloved husband. . . .

"I don't need to tell you that Tony and I have been like brothers since childhood. No brother I have ever had have I been more confidential with or labored more diligently with for the advancement of the Church than with Tony.

"It has been my custom as well as Gusta's to send books as an expression of sympathy to our friends, when a member of the family circle was called by death, and I expect to send you and your children some books, but it is going to be hard to find some good books to send you as I have sent you and Tony all of the books that I am in the habit of sending.

"What a wonderful welcome is in store for your husband when he meets his father and mother, and your father and mother. No son could have a more wonderful welcome, as one who has labored with zeal to accomplish the things that were so dear to the hearts of his parents and your parents, than Anthony W. Ivins for the splendid work he has done in defense of the truth. He has been true all his days."[6]

Heber J. Grant was born 22 November 1856 in Salt Lake City to Jedediah M. Grant and Rachel Ivins. Married Lucy Stringham 1 November 1877. Three wives, twelve children. Ordained an apostle 16 October 1882 at age twenty-five by George Q. Cannon. Ordained President of the Church 23 November 1918 at age sixty-two. Died 14 May 1945 in Salt Lake City at age eighty-eight.

8

"FIND JOY IN MINISTERING TO THE NEEDS OF THE POOR"

George Albert Smith

~

THE WORDS HE LIVED BY

Many of George Albert Smith's friends, both in and out of the Church, felt that his "creed" epitomized his personality and character:

I would be a friend to the friendless and find joy in ministering to the needs of the poor.

I would visit the sick and afflicted and inspire in them a desire for faith to be healed.

I would teach the truth to the understanding and blessing of all mankind.

I would seek out the erring one and try to win him back to a righteous and a happy life.

I would not seek to force people to live up to my ideals, but rather love them into doing the thing that is right.

I would live with the masses and help to solve their problems that their earth life may be happy.

I would avoid the publicity of high positions and discourage flattery of thoughtless friends.

I would not knowingly wound the feelings of any, not even one who may have wronged me, but would seek to do him good and make him my friend.

I would overcome the tendency to selfishness and jealousy and rejoice in the successes of all the children of my Heavenly Father.

I would not be an enemy to any living soul.

Knowing that the Redeemer of mankind has offered to the world the only plan that will fully develop us and make us happy here and hereafter, I feel it not only a duty, but also a blessed privilege to disseminate the truth.[1]

President Smith's friends were not surprised that he emphasized concern for the poor in the first point of his creed. He did so again in his dedicatory prayer for the Idaho Falls Idaho Temple, given on 23 September 1945:

We are most grateful unto Thee that Thou didst inspire Thy servants to institute the Welfare Program of the Church through which it is made possible that the poor and unfortunate might be provided for without the forfeiture of self-respect. May Thy servants continue in Thy favor that they may thereby merit Thy inspiration in developing this Welfare Program until it becomes perfect in all respects to the care and blessing of Thy people.[2]

In subsequent conference addresses President Smith continued with the same emphasis. Here is one example:

This is what the Lord says . . . and I am reading from the fifty-sixth section of the Doctrine and Covenants:

"Wo unto you rich men, that will not give your substance to the poor, for your riches will canker your souls; and this shall be your lamentation in the day of visitation, and of judgment, and of indignation: The harvest is past, the summer is ended, and my soul is not saved!" (D&C 56:16.)

That is what the Lord says of the rich people who refuse to impart of their substance to those who are poor. But he says something just as serious to the poor man who is not doing his best. He says:

"Wo unto you poor men, whose hearts are not broken, whose spirits are not contrite, and whose bellies are not satisfied, and whose hands are not stayed from laying hold upon other men's goods, whose eyes are full of greediness, and who will not labor with your own hands!" (D&C 56:17.) . . .

Now, my brethren and sisters, we have both rich and poor in our organizations. If we are poor, we can be worthy just as the Lord indicates here. We can be pure in heart and do our best, and he will not permit those who do their best to suffer for the necessities of life among the people who are in the Church of Jesus Christ of Latter-day Saints.

Our welfare program has been a wonderful thing, a program by which unemployed may be employed, and a way has been opened for men and women who cannot do much work but who can do something to be gainfully employed. How much better off we are when we are occupied with some reasonable work.

Consider the condition in the world, the number who are determined to take from the rich man not what belongs to themselves, but that which belongs to the others. God has permitted men to get wealth, and if they obtained it properly, it is theirs, and he will bless them in its use if they will use it properly.

I hope we are not going to become bitter because some men

and women are well-to-do. If we are well-to-do, I hope we are not going to be self-centered and unconscious of the needs of our Father's other children. If we are better off than they are, we ought to be real brothers and sisters, not make-believe. Our desires should be to develop in this world such an organization that others, seeing our good works would be constrained to glorify the name of our Heavenly Father.[3]

HE LIVED AS HE TAUGHT

SENDING RELIEF TO THE VICTIMS OF WORLD WAR II

During the October general conference of 1947, seventy-seven-year-old President George Albert Smith stood and related one of the great examples of humanitarian service in the history of the Church:

"It may be of interest to you to know that since World War II closed, more than seventy-five major carloads of food and clothing and bedding have been shipped across the sea to those needy people over there, without any expense to them whatsoever.

"When the war was over, I went representing the Church, to see the president of the United States. When I called on him, he received me very graciously—I had met him before—and I said: 'I have just come to ascertain from you, Mr. President, what your attitude will be if the Latter-day Saints are prepared to ship food and clothing and bedding to Europe.'

"He smiled and looked at me, and said: 'Well, what do you want to ship it over there for? Their money isn't any good.'

"I said: 'We don't want their money.' He looked at me and asked: 'You don't mean you are going to give it to them?'

"I said: 'Of course, we would give it to them. They are our brothers and sisters and are in distress. God has blessed us with a surplus, and we will be glad to send it if we can have the co-operation of the government.'

"He said: 'You are on the right track,' and added, 'we will be glad to help you in any way we can.'

"I have thought of that a good many times. After we had sat there a moment or two, he said again: 'How long will it take you to get this ready?'

"I said: 'It's all ready.'

"The government you remember had been destroying food and refusing to plant grain during the war, so I said to him:

"'Mr. President, while the administration at Washington were advising the destroying of food, we were building elevators and filling them with grain, and increasing our flocks and our herds, and now what we need is the cars and the ships in order to send considerable food, clothing and bedding to the people of Europe who are in distress. We have an organization in the Church that has over two thousand homemade quilts ready.' . . .

"Now, we couldn't have done that a hundred years ago. We were seeking food ourselves. Our people in this valley then were digging thistle and sego roots for food, and they were utilizing every means possible to get food to keep the soul and body together. In a hundred years the desert has been made to blossom as the rose."[4]

With permission to send clothing and other commodities to Europe, the Church announced a special drive to collect the needed items.

As Glenn Rudd, former manager of Welfare Square and long-time member of the General Welfare Committee, writes:

"The members of the Church in America responded by donating large amounts of new and used clothing and other goods. These were received at Welfare Square in the cannery building, where they were sorted and prepared for shipping. The cannery was not being used during the winter that year. The amount that came in almost filled the building. Many people volunteered to help in this effort. . . .

"When the donations were being sorted and packaged, Elder Harold B. Lee and Elder Marion G. Romney took President George Albert Smith to Welfare Square. They observed the generous response of the membership of the Church to the clothing drive and the preparations for sending the goods overseas. Brother Stewart Eccles, who was with the Brethren, reported that tears ran down President Smith's face as he watched the workers package this great volume of donated clothing, shoes, and other goods. After a few moments he removed a new overcoat that he had on and said, 'Please ship this.' The Brethren said to him, 'No, President, don't send that; it's cold and you need your coat.' But President Smith would not take it back. Brother Eccles went into an office and had a secretary type a note to put in the pocket of the overcoat so that the person eventually receiving it would know that it came from the President of the Church. President Smith insisted that he didn't need his coat to go back to the Church Office Building. The brethren helped him get into the warm car and returned him to his office."[5]

"I WANT YOU TO LOOK AFTER THE INDIANS"

George Albert Smith's concern for helping the poor was also evident in his work with the Native Americans. In the fall of 1946, a year and a half after he became President of the Church, President Smith called Elder Spencer W. Kimball, then fifty-one years old, to his office. He handed Elder Kimball several file folders, and said, "I want you to look after the Indians—they are neglected. Take charge and watch after the Indians in all the world."

Accompanied by Elder Matthew Cowley, President Smith and Elder Kimball soon traveled to the Navajo Indian Reservation in Window Rock, Arizona. In the words of President Kimball's biographers: "Almost two hundred white ministers and government officials met in 'Little Washington,' in an octagonal room circled with benches, the chairs set in the center. It seemed strange to Elder Kimball that these missionary sessions began without prayer. For two days the President and the other two apostles sat on the hard wooden outer benches, waiting to tell of the Church's needs in carrying out its program for the Indians. Until the Church was recognized, the missionaries could not rent, buy, or build on the reservation without permission.

"During the second day the chairman gave the ministers the floor. One after another stood and attacked the Mormons, demanding that they be kept off the reservation. One complained about two elders who had visited and administered to hospitalized Indians of his flock. He insisted that missionaries be restricted to their own members. Complaints strung on and on. Finally President George Albert Smith, out on the edge of the room, stood and was given the floor.

"'My friends,' he said, 'I am perplexed and shocked. I thought it would please me very much if any good Christian missionary of any denomination would be kind enough to visit me and bind up my wounds and pour on the sacred oil. My great, kind friends, we're all brothers and sisters, all children of our Heavenly Father. We only want to bless your people.' To Elder Kimball 'it was like fire and cleansed.' President Smith's approach laid the groundwork for a more tolerant attitude toward the Mormon missionaries."[6]

Due to President Smith's foresight and charitable manner, Elder Kimball was able to report the next year: "A year ago we established down in Blanding, Utah, a small school, somewhat as an experiment. It has been very successful. With an outlay of only $1,500 total, we have built and equipped a two-room schoolhouse there under the direction of Brother Albert R. Lyman, who has done a glorious work. There have been many donations of all kinds, in materials, in food, in clothing. For the first year they fed these little Indian children, twenty-seven of them, a warm midday meal, clothed them, and taught them not only the three R's but the gospel. It has been very successful, and we are delighted with the prospects that are ahead of us for the second year now, which is beginning. I visited this school last year when it was in session. I noticed that three of the Indian women came, one of whom had five children, four in the school and one in the cradle upon her back. She sat at the sewing machine all day long in one corner of the larger schoolroom, and frequently we would see her going over to one of the little desks, kneeling down beside it to help her children to learn, and to impress upon them the importance of taking advantage of this unusual opportunity which many thousands of little boys and girls should, but do not have."[7]

George Albert Smith was born 4 April 1870 in Salt Lake City to John Henry Smith and Sarah Farr. Married Lucy Woodruff 25 May 1892. Three children. Ordained an apostle 8 October 1903 at age thirty-three by Joseph F. Smith. Ordained President of the Church 21 May 1945 at age seventy-five. Died 4 April 1951, his eighty-first birthday, in Salt Lake City.

9

"IF YOU WOULD HAVE FRIENDS, BE ONE"

David O. McKay

THE WORDS HE LIVED BY

In a list reminiscent of George Albert Smith's personal creed, David O. McKay offered his ten rules for happiness:

1. Develop yourself by self-discipline.

2. Joy comes through creation—sorrow through destruction. Every living thing can grow; use the world wisely to realize soul growth.

3. Do things which are hard to do.

4. Entertain upbuilding thoughts. What you think about when you do not have to think shows what you really are.

5. Do your best this hour, and you will do better the next.

6. Be true to those who trust you.

7. Pray for wisdom, courage, and a kind heart.

8. Give heed to God's messages through inspiration. If self-indulgence, jealousy, avarice, or worry have deadened your response, pray to the Lord to wipe out these impediments.

9. True friends enrich life. If you would have friends, be one.

10. Faith is the foundation of all things—including happiness.[1]

While President McKay exemplified all of these principles, he is particularly remembered as one who built friendships throughout the world, gaining the trust of such diverse people as the famed minister Norman Vincent Peale, U.S. President Lyndon Johnson, movie producer Cecil B. DeMille, and the queen of the Netherlands.

"Another element of life at its best is the joy of friends," wrote President McKay. "Man is truly a social being and cannot live by himself alone. 'All that he sends into the hearts of others comes back into his own.' There are few things in life sweeter than friendship, declared by someone to be 'the gift of the Gods, the most precious boon to man.'"[2]

He again emphasized the value of friendship when he said:

> Among life's sweetest blessings is fellowship with men and women whose ideals and aspirations are high and noble. Next to a sense of kinship with God come the helpfulness, encouragement, and inspiration of friends. Friendship is a sacred possession. As air, water, and sunshine to flowers, trees, and verdure, so smiles, sympathy, and love of friends to the daily life of man! "To live, laugh, love one's friends, and be loved by them is to bask in the sunshine of life."

One of the principal reasons which the Lord had for establishing his Church is to give all persons high and low, rich and poor, strong and feeble an opportunity to associate with their fellow men in an atmosphere of uplifting, religious fellowship. This may be found in priesthood quorums, auxiliaries, sacrament meetings. He who neglects these opportunities, who fails to take advantage of them, to that extent starves his own soul.

I am happy in my love for my immediate associates, President George Albert Smith and President J. Reuben Clark, Jr., and for these noble men of the Council of the Twelve, the Patriarch, the Assistants to the Council of the Twelve, the Council of the Seventy, the Presiding Bishopric. I find it a joy to work with you loyal men who preside in stakes and wards and branches. It is a privilege to have the opportunity to labor with you, to recognize your unselfish devotion to the Church.[3]

HE LIVED AS HE TAUGHT

The Enduring Friendship of David O. McKay and Stephen L Richards

When he was attending the University of Utah in the late 1890s, young David O. McKay, who played on the football team and became president of his class, may have made the acquaintance of a fellow student by the name of Stephen L Richards. Six years David's junior, Stephen was the grandson of Willard Richards, apostle and friend of Joseph Smith. Like David, Stephen savored the academic life and excelled at it. After his graduation, he married Irene Merrill, and they departed for the Malad Valley in Idaho.

"The young husband felled and hauled the logs which became their first dwelling, and the young wife made it into an attractive home. . . . Hay in the Malad Valley brought three dollars a ton and grain forty cents a bushel when delivered to the shipping point at Collinston, Utah. But the small family lived comfortably, if modestly, from the ranch and from supplemental earnings Brother Richards made as principal of the Malad public school."[4]

After two years in Malad, Stephen made good on a goal to attend law school. He graduated *cum laude* from the first class at the University of Chicago Law School. The dean at the law school later said that Stephen was the most capable student he had been associated with.

Stephen and Irene returned to Utah, where Stephen opened private practice, taught at the University of Utah Law School, and served as Murray City attorney. In 1906, when he was twenty-seven, he was called to the general board of the Deseret Sunday School Union. Of this calling, Gordon B. Hinckley later wrote: "There he became acquainted with a young school principal from Ogden, a man who six months earlier had been sustained a member of the Council of the Twelve and who now was named a member of the general superintendency of the Sunday School Union. There and then commenced a David-and-Jonathan friendship which has lasted and strengthened during all the intervening years, and which culminated in April 1951 when President David O. McKay chose Stephen L Richards to be his counselor in the First Presidency. It is a tribute to both of them that they have worked together so long and under such a variety of circumstances and that their love and appreciation for one another has grown steadily over the years."[5]

David and Stephen shared a love and enthusiasm for education and a dedication to the gospel. The friendship between these kindred spirits grew as time passed. In 1909, when general Sunday School assistant superintendent George Reynolds died, general Sunday School superintendent Joseph F. Smith—also serving as

President of the Church—called David as first assistant and Stephen as second assistant. The three men formed a strong bond, and President Smith learned firsthand of Stephen's analytical and organizational abilities. Then, when Quorum of the Twelve president Francis M. Lyman died late in 1916, President Smith named Stephen L Richards to fill the vacancy in the Quorum. Thirty-seven-year-old Stephen accepted the call and gave up his promising law career. "On that occasion [Stephen's call to the Twelve]," said Elder McKay, "every mind assented and every heart testified that the Lord had spoken, and that he had indeed called into the service of the apostleship a 'chosen vessel.'"[6]

"I found that this man had the happy faculty of being able to analyze a problem thoroughly, seemingly not overlooking any possible contingency," wrote Joseph Anderson, longtime secretary to the President of the Church. "He had an astute, analytical mind, great wisdom and capacity, and his judgment was dependable. Perhaps he had attained these skills by a native intelligence highly trained in the legal profession. . . . As both an apostle and a member of the First Presidency, President Richards was not easily swayed from a decision once he had reached a conclusion that his analysis of the problem at hand was right."[7]

David and Stephen served together in the Quorum of the Twelve from 1917 to 1934, when David was called as second counselor to President Heber J. Grant. In addition, when David was named general Sunday School superintendent, he selected Stephen as his first counselor. Their friendship continued to blossom. Then in 1951, President George Albert Smith's health began to fail. One week after he died, his successor David O. McKay spoke at the solemn assembly:

"It is just one week ago today that the realization came to me that this responsibility of leadership would probably fall upon my shoulders. I received word that President George Albert Smith had taken a turn for the worse, and that the doctor thought the end was not far off. I hastened to his bedside, and with his weeping daughters, son, and other kinfolk, I entered his sickroom. For the first time, he failed to recognize me.

"Then I had to accept the realization that the Lord had chosen not to answer our pleadings as we would have had them answered, and that he was going to take him home to himself. . . . Several days preceding that visit, as President Clark and I were considering problems of import pertaining to the Church, he, ever solicitous of the welfare of the Church and of my feelings, would say, 'The responsibility will be yours to make this decision,' but each time I would refuse to face what to him seemed a reality."[8]

Surprising no one, President McKay selected Stephen L Richards and J. Reuben Clark as his counselors. Some were surprised, however, that Stephen was named first counselor. President McKay addressed this issue directly:

"I am prompted to say a word in answer to a question which undoubtedly is in every one of your minds. . . .

"When a President is chosen and sustained (that includes the president of the Aaronic Priesthood who is the Bishop of a Ward, also Presidents of quorums or superintendents or presidents of auxiliaries) it is the practice of the Church to let the president name his counselors.

"Anticipating that the Council of the Twelve would grant to me that same privilege, I thoughtfully and prayerfully considered what two men would be most helpful and most contributive to the advancement of the Church. The impression came, I am sure, directly from Him whose Church this is, and who presides over it, that the two counselors whom you have this day approved should be the other members of the quorum of the First Presidency. . . .

"I chose these two members from the Council of the Twelve— two men with whom I have labored closely for many years, whose worth, whose ability I know. I have been associated with Elder Richards directly in Church affairs and in presiding positions for over thirty years. I have been associated with President Clark in two quorums of the First Presidency for over sixteen years. With these and other facts in mind, the question arose as to the order they should occupy in this new quorum.

"Each man I love. Each man is capable in his particular lines, and particularly with respect to the welfare and advancement of the Kingdom of God.

"I realized that there would be a question in the minds of some as to which one of the two should be chosen as first counselor. That question resolved itself in my mind first as to the order of precedence, seniority in the Council of the Twelve Apostles. That should make no difference according to the practice of the Church, because members of the Council had heretofore been chosen irrespective of the position a member occupied in the Council of the Twelve. And, as I have already said, high priests have been chosen even as first counselors who were not members of the Council.

"I felt that one guiding principle in this choice would be to follow the seniority in the Council. These two men were sitting in their places in that presiding body in the Church, and I felt impressed that it would be advisable to continue that same seniority in the new quorum of the First Presidency. I repeat, not as an established policy, but because it seemed advisable in view of my close relationship to these two choice leaders. . . .

". . . Neither should you feel that there is any demotion. President Clark is a wonderful servant. You have had demonstrated here this morning his ability in carrying out details, and he is just that efficient in everything pertaining to the work.

"You should understand further, that in the counselorship of the Quorum of the First Presidency these two men are coordinate in authority, in love, and confidence, in freedom to make suggestions, and recommendations, and in their responsibility not only to the Quorum but also to the Lord Jesus Christ and to the people generally.

"They are two great men. I love them both, and say God bless them, and give you the assurance that there will be harmony and love and confidence in the Quorum of the First Presidency as you have sustained them today."[9]

President Richards responded humbly:

"I call upon the Lord to come to my rescue in this, the most trying hour of my life. It reaches beyond my understanding to know why I have been privileged in the providence of God to stand before you, my brethren and sisters of the Church, in the capacity in which I have this day been presented to you."

He also paid tribute to his friend David O. McKay:

"For more than forty-five years I have had a great man as a friend. I don't know how I have deserved his friendship as he has given it to me. His friendship has been one of the main factors of encouragement in my life. My association with him has brought more richness into my life and my experience than any other association outside that of my own flesh and blood.

"This great man has stimulated me in times of discouragement to go forward and give the best I could to this work. I shall never live long enough to pay the debt of gratitude I owe my friend. I respond to his call with the deepest humility, with a great sense of inadequacy, but with an obligation to give to him my best.

"One of the few ways in which I can account for this which has transpired lies in another friendship. My grandfather, Willard Richards, was an intimate and close friend of the Prophet Joseph

Smith. I am honored to learn and to know that the Prophet prized his friendship, and is said to have remarked on one occasion that no one could ever have a finer friend than was Willard Richards. . . .

"I have often felt that the only reason for my being in the presiding councils of the Church is in the devotion of Willard Richards to the Prophet Joseph Smith. . . . I would like to be as true a friend to President David O. McKay as my grandfather was to the Prophet, and in some measure show to him my appreciation of his marvelous kindness to me."[10]

President McKay responded similarly: "His loyalty to [the Sunday School board] and to the cause has won their loyalty to him; his gentlemanly and courteous consideration of their thoughts and feelings, his unselfish devotion to the truth, and his invincible determination to choose the right have merited their abiding confidence and high esteem."[11]

Although President Richards had suffered heart problems for many years, his vitality seemed to increase after his call to the First Presidency, and he was able to work hard. He also lengthened his service by being able to relax when occasion demanded it.

As Joseph Anderson said: "This man gave to President McKay and to his position as a counselor in the First Presidency his every ounce of energy, even frequently when he was not well. He was completely devoted to his old friend and to the Church. President McKay relied wholeheartedly on his judgment, particularly in financial and missionary matters, and he leaned heavily upon him."[12]

President Richards had been at his office regularly when he suddenly died of a heart attack on 19 May 1959. He was seventy-nine years old. Eighty-five-year-old David O. McKay offered an emotional farewell at the funeral of his close friend of more than fifty years. "Goodbye for the present, Stephen L, my beloved friend and associate. We shall miss you—Oh! how we shall miss you!—but we shall continue to carry on until we meet again."[13]

"BROTHER McKAY, THERE WAS NO VEIL"

David O. McKay and Hugh J. Cannon shared an experience that had a powerful effect on the history of the Church. The son of George Q. Cannon (who had served as a counselor to Brigham Young, John Taylor, Wilford Woodruff, and Lorenzo Snow), Hugh was three years older than David. He had served as president of the German Mission from 1901 to 1905. During the period from 1909 to 1920, Hugh and David had become friends as they served in the Deseret Sunday School Union together. (Stephen L Richards was one of their co-workers in the Sunday School.)

Late in 1920, President Heber J. Grant called forty-seven-year-old David O. McKay, then a member of the Quorum of the Twelve, and fifty-year-old Hugh J. Cannon, president of the Salt Lake City Liberty Stake and editor of the *Improvement Era*, on an unprecedented world tour of Church missions. Bidding their families farewell, the two friends departed on 4 December 1920. Their accounts of the journey make it clear that their casual friendship blossomed into a deep and lasting bond as they visited Saints and missionaries across the globe.

Onboard a ship from San Francisco to Japan, they quickly discovered that seasickness would be a regular part of their long journey. After the first night, David was feeling queasy but noted that "Hugh J. returned from breakfast looking as robust and rosy as an athlete, and smacking his lips in appreciation of an excellent meal. . . . As he looked at me, I fancied I saw spreading over his countenance indications of a laugh he was trying hard to suppress. I said

71

something which enabled him to lift the lid and let off his mirthful steam."[14]

David ventured on deck only to hurry back to his cabin, later finding humor in his miserable situation: "Good-bye last night's dinner! Good-bye yesterday's Rotary luncheon! And during the next sixty hours, good-bye everything I had ever eaten since I was a babe on mother's knee. I'm not sure I didn't even cross the threshold into the pre-existent state."[15]

In Japan, the two men noticed that Japanese people on the streetcar habitually stood and offered them seats. "We concluded it was because we were foreigners," David wrote, "and were even more grateful; but about the fifth or sixth time, it suddenly dawned on me that these people were giving us seats because they thought us two old men!" Hugh agreed, adding with his characteristic humor that David had "always been the first to be given consideration."[16]

From Japan, the two companions traveled to Korea, Manchuria, and China. In Peking, David felt inspired to dedicate China for the preaching of the gospel. Hugh recorded this sacred experience in detail: "With no definite goal in mind, we left the hotel and walked through the legation quarter, under the shadow of dear Old Glory, out into what is known as 'The Forbidden City,' past the crumbling temples reared to an 'Unknown God.' Directed, as we believe, by a Higher Power, we came to a grove of cypress trees, partially surrounded by a moat, and walked to its extreme northwest corner, then retraced our steps until reaching a tree with divided trunk which had attracted our attention when we first saw it.

"'This is the spot,' said Elder McKay.

"A reposeful peace hovered over the place which seemed already hallowed. . . . Elder David O. McKay, in the authority of the Holy Apostleship, dedicated and set apart the Chinese Realm for the preaching of the gospel of the Lord Jesus Christ, whenever the

Church authorities shall deem it advisable to send out missionaries for that purpose. Never was the power of his calling more apparent in his utterances. He blessed the land and its benighted people, and supplicated the Almighty to acknowledge this blessing. . . .

"It was such a prayer and blessing as must be recognized in heaven, and though the effects may not be suddenly apparent, they will be none the less real."[17]

"God was with us when we stood beneath that tree in old China and turned the key for the preaching of the gospel in the Chinese realm," Elder McKay later said in a general conference address. "My words may not convince you of the fact, but no disputant can convince us that our souls were not filled to overflowing with the Spirit of God on that occasion."[18]

Next they sailed to Hawaii and visited the site where George Q. Cannon had baptized the first Hawaiian convert. Also present was E. Wesley Smith, son of Joseph F. Smith, who had also served in Hawaii as a missionary. The occasion was particularly significant to Hugh and Wesley because both of their fathers had since passed away (George Q. Cannon in 1901 and Joseph F. Smith in 1918). As Elder McKay offered a prayer, a Hawaiian member of the Church saw two men join the group and shake hands with each other. After a moment, the two men disappeared. The Hawaiian, Brother Kailimai, told the group that the two men he had seen looked much like Hugh and Wesley.

"I think it was George Q. Cannon and Joseph F. Smith, two missionaries to Hawaii, whom that spiritual-minded man saw," said Elder McKay. He turned to Brother Kailimai and added, "I do not understand the significance of your vision, but I do know that the veil between us and those former missionaries was very thin."

With tears in his eyes, Hugh said, "Brother McKay, there was no veil."[19]

After returning to the mainland briefly, David and Hugh sailed to Tahiti, New Zealand, and Samoa. Of their last meeting with the Samoan Saints, David wrote: "As we came out, we found the people standing in a double column from our door out across the lawn into the street. They had prepared a farewell song for us and all began to sing. As we passed through the lines, shaking hands with them, sobs interrupted the singing. Staunch old Papo, the head of the village, sobbed like a child, and clung to us as though we were his sons. As we mounted our horses, we looked back and saw the crowd, headed by the band, coming toward us for one more parting handshake."[20]

Because of fear over measles, the Tongan government required all visitors to be quarantined on a small island for fourteen days before visiting Tonga. As Elder McKay's son later wrote, "Rather than miss the Tongan Mission, it was decided that Brother Cannon should continue to New Zealand and father would go into quarantine."

"I felt pretty lonesome at parting from Brother Cannon and gloomy at the prospects ahead," wrote David.[21]

Next came Australia. "From Australia they moved through Southeast Asia into lands overflowing with hungry and haggard faces, exemplified by the beggar who died near where Elder McKay was standing on a street in India. The hot, sticky boat ride from India to Egypt provided more time for the two missionaries to think of home and family. One evening Elder McKay sat on deck next to a lady who was exhausted from jostling her little boy to keep him from crying. Elder McKay smiled at her, then asked if he could hold the child while she rested. She gladly consented, and soon the boy was asleep in the Apostle's arms."[22]

One day on the ship Hugh yelled to David to come see a shark. "Nobody needed a second invitation," recalled David. "I saw him

74

just as the sailors had pulled him over the deck railing. A hook, the size of a bailing hook was in his jaw. . . . They tied both ropes, stretched the monster out, and struck him a blow on the nose which was supposed to kill him instantly. . . .

"Thinking he was dead, I began to examine him, and took hold of his fins. He gave a sudden lurch that loosed his tail with which he gave me a blow on the legs that gave me a sensation I shall not soon forget."[23] One can imagine David's reaction to this—and his friend Hugh's.

They next traveled to Palestine and several nearby locations. They met with a small group of Saints, and the Spirit of the Lord was powerfully present. These Saints were living in poor conditions, and the two elders were able to help them by distributing funds from a special fast held in Utah.

The last leg of the journey came when David and Hugh visited missions in Europe. By the time they arrived home, on Christmas Eve of 1921 (more than a year after they departed), they had traveled an amazing 24,277 miles by land and 32,819 miles by water, experiencing a mission like no two other companions ever had. Through humor, sickness, endless days of travel, and one sacred experience after another, the two men formed a unique and lasting bond. "When President Grant suggested Brother Cannon as my companion," David said, "I readily acquiesced, because I knew his worth. Then I respected him; today I love him. I think that conveys to you the fact that our more than twelve months' constant companionship, night and day, was most genial and happy."[24]

David's friend Hugh presided over the Swiss-German Mission from 1925 to 1928, dying at the relatively young age of sixty-one in 1931. David, of course, became Church president in 1951.

"During this trip, [David O. McKay] had powerful revelatory experiences concerning the future of the Church worldwide. In

1922 he was called as president of the European Mission, where he showed a remarkable ability to improve the Church's image through positive public relations. . . . President McKay's administration was marked by incredible growth. Church membership tripled, the missionary force grew sixfold, and for the first time temples were erected in Europe (Switzerland, 1955) and the South Pacific (New Zealand, 1958). Under his direction, films were used to present the temple ceremony in various languages. President McKay traveled more miles than all of his predecessors combined."[25]

As he traveled the world as Church president, David O. McKay must have looked back fondly at his remarkable journey with Hugh J. Cannon, a dear friend from younger days.

———————————

David O. McKay was born 8 September 1873 in Huntsville, Utah, to David McKay and Jeanette Evans. Married Emma Ray Riggs 2 January 1901. Seven children. Ordained an apostle 9 April 1906 at age thirty-two by Joseph F. Smith. Sustained as President of the Church 9 April 1951 at age seventy-seven. Died 18 January 1970 in Salt Lake City at age ninety-six.

10

"INGRATITUDE IS ONE OF THE GREATEST OF ALL SINS"

Joseph Fielding Smith

THE WORDS HE LIVED BY

Joseph Fielding Smith was ninety-three years old when he became President of the Church, the oldest man to do so. Throughout his long, productive life, he displayed the qualities of gratitude and humility. As his secretary of fifty years, Ruby Egbert, wrote: "He wouldn't think of asking you to do something for him that he could do himself. . . . He shakes hands with everyone on the elevator and on the floor where his office is. And the door to his office has always been open to anyone who needed his help. . . . He loves children. He has a special voice for them, and will often go out in the hall to play with them or chat with them when they pass."[1]

President Smith felt that the sin of ingratitude brought serious consequences:

> All through their sojourn in the wilderness, Israel showed the disposition of spoiled children. They evidently failed to comprehend the teachings of the Lord that were given to Moses. Therefore when the time came for Israel to cross the Jordan and enter into their inheritance, the prophetic warning the Lord had given them was fulfilled as recorded in the Book of Numbers.
>
> "And the Lord spake unto Moses and unto Aaron, saying,
>
> "How long shall I bear with this evil congregation, which murmur against me? I have heard the murmurings of the children of Israel, which they murmur against me. . . .
>
> "Doubtless ye shall not come into the land, concerning which I sware to make you dwell therein, save Caleb the son of Jephunneh, and Joshua the son of Nun. . . .
>
> "But as for you, your carcases, they shall fall in this wilderness.
>
> "And your children shall wander in the wilderness forty years, and bear your whoredoms, until your carcases be wasted in the wilderness." (Numbers 14:26–33.)[2]

President Smith believed that "the sin of ingratitude . . . [was] the most prevalent of all sins, for we are all guilty of it; I am, you are, the people everywhere upon the face of the earth are guilty of this sin in some degree. . . .

> Now, when we stop to think that the Son of God created this world; all things, the scriptures say, were made by him, and when we think that he came to this world with that mission which he accepted before he was born in Bethlehem, and by the shedding of his blood gave us life that we might rise in the resurrection to live forever; and when he, by the shedding of his blood has offered unto us the remission of our sins and eternal life, through

obedience to the gospel—do you not think that we owe him something in return? We owe him everything. . . .

Now, he has asked us to keep his commandments. He says they are not grievous, and there are so many of us who are not willing to do it. I am speaking now generally of the people of the earth. We are not willing to do it. That certainly is ingratitude. We are ungrateful. Every member of this Church that violates the Sabbath day, that is not honest in the paying of his tithing, that will not keep the Word of Wisdom, that wilfully violates any of the other commandments the Lord has given us, is ungrateful to the Son of God and when ungrateful to the Son of God is ungrateful to the Father who sent him. If our Savior would do so much for us, how in the world is it that we are not willing to abide by his commandments which are not grievous, which do not cause us any suffering if we will only keep them? And yet, people break the Word of Wisdom; they refuse to attend to their duties as officers and members in the Church; many of them stay away from meetings the Lord has called upon them to support. They follow their own desires if they are in conflict with the commandments of the Lord.

If we understood our position and we loved the Lord our God with all our heart, with all our soul, and with all our mind, . . . then we would keep his commandments; when we will not do this, I tell you, my brethren and sisters, we show ingratitude to Jesus Christ."[3]

HE LIVED AS HE TAUGHT

GRATITUDE FOR A SON'S GOOD LIFE

On 2 January 1945 Joseph Fielding Smith, then sixty-eight years old and a widower for the second time, received tragic news from the War Department: his son Lewis had been killed in an airplane crash somewhere over western Africa. Twenty-six-year-old Lewis, who had earlier served a mission in Europe, was a staff sergeant serving with the Army Intelligence Service.

"This word came to us as a most severe shock as we had high hopes that soon he would be back in the United States," Elder Smith wrote in his journal. "We had felt that he would be protected as he has escaped several times before from danger. It was hard for us to realize that such a thing could happen."[4]

Lewis's death came as a double blow because he was the son of Joseph's second wife, Ethel Reynolds, who also had died early, only seven years before. She had died at the young age of forty-seven after suffering a severe illness.

Despite his grief, Elder Smith found reasons to be grateful and hopeful. "If Lewis ever did or said a mean thing I never heard of it," he wrote. "His thoughts were pure as were his actions. . . . As severe as the blow is we have the peace and happiness of knowing that he was clean and free from the vices so prevalent in the world and found in the army. He was true to his faith and is worthy of a glorious resurrection, when we shall be reunited again."[5]

A letter soon arrived from Lewis's commanding officer, a Lieutenant Garland F. Smith, and other letters from several of Lewis's friends in the military. The letters offered Joseph and his family further reason to be thankful for Lewis's life. In a letter to his daughter and son-in-law, Lois and William S. Fife, Joseph wrote: "We got further word about Lewis from one of his companions, Gene F. Walburn. He gave us the information regarding the accident to the plane and said the bodies were taken to Maiduguri, Nigeria, and buried in a 'beautiful military cemetery' there. One thing that helps us is the fact that each of the men who has written to us has testified to Lewis' clean life, his high principles and his integrity to his religion. When each writes this way, without any consultation, it is a great tribute to our boy, son and brother. . . . Such words as these are comforting, and each has testified in the same manner about him. The beautiful thing about it all is that it is so true. A better boy could not be found. A more worthy one could not be taken. We are sure that he was called to some work on the other side."[6]

THE BEAUTIFUL VOICE AND SPIRIT OF JESSIE EVANS SMITH

Seven years before Lewis's death, Joseph Fielding Smith had shown a similar spirit when dealing with Ethel's death. "If I should ever die before you," she had said to Joseph, "I want you to have Jessie Evans sing at my funeral." Following these wishes, Joseph asked Sister Evans, a well-known contralto soloist with the Mormon Tabernacle Choir, to sing at the funeral. Afterwards, Joseph found reason to be grateful and sent a letter of appreciation to Jessie:

"Words at times are feeble things in conveying the true feelings of the soul. I greatly appreciate your kindness to me and mine in the services yesterday. You have done much on occasions of this kind to comfort and bless those in tribulation, and your willingness to aid in such cases has long been noted by me. You have been kind to the members of my family before, and I wish you to know that the service so given has been fully appreciated by me. I always enjoy your singing, as much as any person I have ever heard. I trust you will pardon me for saying this, for it is a heartfelt expression. May the Lord bless you and reward you with the fulness of his blessings, now and forever. This I humbly pray."[7]

Jessie responded to the letter, and a friendship soon developed. Several months later, Joseph and Jessie were married in the

Salt Lake Temple by President Heber J. Grant. Over the next thirty-three years, much of which President Smith was serving as president of the Quorum of the Twelve, they traveled throughout the world together. "While he was primarily a speaker and she a singer, they each did some of the other as well: she sometimes spoke as well as sang, and by and by he began singing duets with her, singing the alto part in his second-tenor voice. The congregations loved it. Once in awhile they would sing one of the songs that he had written. One of the songs they sang most frequently together was 'If I Knew You and You Knew Me.' They thoroughly enjoyed singing together, and spent many a pleasant hour at home practicing and singing for their own amusement, as well as singing in public."[8]

JOSEPH FIELDING SMITH'S FINAL DAYS

Joseph Fielding Smith taught one of his most powerful lessons about gratitude at the close of his life. He was ninety-five years old when he spoke at the April general conference in 1972. His short, sincere address focused on gratitude:

"My dear brethren and sisters: I feel that the Lord has been with us in all the sessions of this conference; that we have been fed the bread of life; and that we are better prepared now to be the kind of people the Lord would have us be.

"I am grateful to all of the Brethren for their wise counsel and for the messages they delivered as they were guided by the power of the Spirit.

"I think we should conclude on a tone of thanksgiving, of blessing, and of testimony.

"I have no language to convey the feelings of thanksgiving which are in my heart for the infinite and eternal blessings the Lord has given to me, to my family, to the Church, and, in fact, to the whole world.

"I am grateful for the atoning sacrifice of the Son of God—that because of his suffering and death all men shall be raised in immortality, while those who believe and obey his laws shall have eternal life in his kingdom.

"I am thankful for the restoration of eternal truth in this final gospel dispensation; for the mission and ministry of Joseph Smith, the Prophet, and my grandfather, Hyrum Smith, the Patriarch; and for the fact that the keys of the kingdom of God have been committed again to man on the earth.

"I am pleased with the growth and development of the Church, with the increased missionary work, with the many temples we now have, and with the lives of all those who are seeking to serve the Lord.

"I pray that the Lord will bless all the members of the Church; and by virtue of the keys and power which I hold, I bless the Saints—those who dwell in the household of faith, those who love and seek the Lord.

"What a glorious thing it is to have the saving truths of the everlasting gospel, to be members of 'the only true and living church upon the face of the whole earth' (D&C 1:30), to be on the path leading to eternal life in our Father's kingdom!

"O God our Heavenly and Eternal Father, look down in love and in mercy upon this thy church and upon the members of the church who keep thy commandments. Let thy Spirit dwell in our hearts forever; and when the trials and woes of this life are over, may we return to their presence, with our loved ones, and dwell in thy house forever, I humbly pray, in the name of Jesus Christ. Amen."[9]

This was President Smith's last conference address. His

biographers noted that three months later, on Sunday, 2 July 1972, "President Smith ate a light supper with the McConkies at 7:30 P.M. Then he relaxed in his favorite chair, a large comfortable black vinyl recliner that had been brought from his apartment especially for his enjoyment. It was the chair that Jessie had been sitting in when she died 11 months ago. Oh, what a lonely 11 months that had been without her. How terribly he missed her. And how he missed Louie and Ethel, and his son Lewis and other loved ones who had departed this life. And yet, how fortunate he was to have such good devoted children to look after him and comfort and help him in his old age and loneliness. . . .

"Amelia and Bruce and their youngsters had done all possible to make him feel welcome in their home. They had brought not only his favorite chair and some other pieces of furniture up for his use, but a collection of his favorite books. As he conversed Sunday evening with Amelia *he again expressed his love and appreciation for her.* . . .

"While visiting with her father Amelia was also writing a letter to one of her children. At about 9:20 P.M. she left the living room for a minute or two to get an address she needed.

"'When Amelia returned,' reported Bruce, 'she found her father in what seemed to be a state of shock. She called to me, and within moments, not more than a few seconds at most, we were giving him oxygen—to no avail. It was apparent his time had come and that the tenement of clay no longer housed the eternal spirit.

"'His passing was as sweet and easy, as calm and as peaceful as though he had fallen asleep, which in fact he had. . . . Truly when the Lord took his prophet, there was no sting. President Smith did not taste of death.'"[10]

Joseph Fielding Smith's final days and final hours were consistent with the pattern he had established long before. He truly showed a remarkable sense of gratitude throughout the entirety of his long and productive life.

Joseph Fielding Smith was born 19 July 1876 in Salt Lake City to Joseph F. Smith and Julina Lambson. Married Louie E. Shurtliff 26 April 1898. Two children. (She died 30 March 1908.) Married Ethel G. Reynolds 2 November 1908. Nine children. (She died 26 August 1937.) Married Jessie Ella Evans 12 April 1938. (She died 14 November 1970.) Ordained an apostle 7 April 1910 at age thirty-three by his father Joseph F. Smith. Ordained President of the Church 23 January 1970 at age ninety-three. Died 2 July 1972 in Salt Lake City at age ninety-five.

11

"MAKE EACH DAY YOUR MASTERPIECE"

THE WORDS HE LIVED BY

Harold B. Lee was a man who lived life to the fullest. In 1930, when the United States was reeling from the Great Depression, Harold was called—as the youngest stake president in the Church—to preside over the Pioneer Stake in Salt Lake City. He performed his responsibilities with such fervor and efficiency that in the mid-1930s he was called as the first managing director of the Church Welfare Program. Six years after that came a call as an apostle.

Both as a member of the Quorum of the Twelve and as President of the Church, Harold B. Lee frequently admonished the Saints to make the most of their opportunities:

As with every day of your life, you can never relive any part
of it except in memory; and if any day be wasted or misspent, that
day becomes only one of regret and remorse. To live one's life to
the fullest, then, becomes a daily responsibility for which you
need the constant guidance of divine powers to avoid the pitfalls
that make for long detours back onto the path of safety and
truth.[1]

You are equipped with strong bodies and educated minds.
Add to these an unshakable faith in a divine providence and you
have the tools by which you may build a successful life. Make
each day your masterpiece and live so nobly that you may witness
honestly each day: Whatever came to your hand this day, you did
it to the best of your ability.[2]

For President Lee, living each day to its fullest was closely
linked to attaining true joy in this life:

"Man is, that he might have joy" (see 2 Nephi 2:25) is a saying now centuries old, but before any of us can achieve the highest of our possibilities, we must realize that the true joy of living is
not attained except by him who likewise sees his life "as a beginning, as an introduction of what is to follow, the entrance into
that immeasurable extent of being which is the true life of man."

It should be clear to any reasoning mind that thoughtfully
ponders these matters that each of us has the responsibility of
building a life, not just for the period of our mortal existence, to
molder or crumble as clay into the dust when we die. Rather, we
are laying the cornerstones here and now for that larger extent of
being which does not end with death. Only when our lives are
measuring up to the best we know, despite unfortunate and trying situations, only then have we conquered self and are realizing
the joy of living which is the purpose of existence.[3]

Not surprisingly, President Lee saw happiness as being closely linked to selfless service:

> There's the secret of your happiness in life when you analyze it, to learn to live outside yourself in love.[4]
>
> The person who is thinking of others and doing for others is happy. Happiness lies in that little kindness we do when we don't expect anything in return.[5]

Joy and happiness are also linked to remembering and trusting in God:

> When a man leans to his own understanding and boasts by his own strength—when he boasts of probing the mysteries of the atom or the depth of the sea or the secrets of outer space—he forgets God and claims he is his own master, [and] the result is untold suffering. Even though one's position is maintained, even though material wealth increases, a success quickly turns to failure when God has been forgotten. There is no peace of mind, no personal satisfaction of inward joy. To "trust in the Lord with all thine heart" (Proverbs 3:5) is a mark of strength and is the only path to happiness, success, and true fulfillment.[6]

HE LIVED AS HE TAUGHT

THE HISTORIC JOURNEY OF HAROLD B. LEE AND GORDON B. HINCKLEY

President Harold B. Lee's determination to make each day a masterpiece was evident in a historic trip he made to the Holy Land with Elder Gordon B. Hinckley. When President Lee, then seventy-three years old and Church president for a short two months, announced his intention to visit Israel in September of 1972, some of the brethren were in tears as they expressed concern for President Lee's safety, especially since it had only been days since Arab terrorists had killed several Israelis at the Olympics in Munich, Germany. Violence or warfare in Israel seemed likely. Still, President Lee felt strongly that he should visit the Holy Land, which would make him the first Church president to do so. Elder Hinckley, then sixty-two, was to be his companion.

President Lee and Elder Hinckley and their wives flew to London and immediately began a grueling schedule. Lord Thomson of Fleet, an influential newspaper owner, invited them to a luncheon where several prominent British citizens were present. Later that same day, at the London Temple, President Lee gave the sealing powers to seven brethren and held an impromptu meeting requested by stake presidents in the area. President Lee and Elder Hinckley both spoke to more than six hundred Saints.

The next day, Lord Thompson hosted another high-level luncheon, this one bringing together key religious leaders of the Jewish, Catholic, and Protestant churches of England. Next came a press conference with reporters from the leading papers in London. Rather than getting much-needed rest that evening, President and Sister Lee and Elder and Sister Hinckley met with four hundred missionaries.

The next day, after visiting the British Museum and seeing such famous objects as the Rosetta Stone and artifacts relating to King Tutankhamen, Elder Hinckley reorganized the London Stake presidency. He chose John Henry Cox, only thirty-one years old, as the new president. When he expressed possible concern over President Cox's youth, President Lee handed him a note that read, "I was thirty-one when I became a stake president."[7]

The journey continued as the party flew to Greece. Though President Lee experienced back pain during the night, the group, now accompanied by International Mission President Edwin Q. Cannon and his wife, rose early to visit Mars Hill, site of the Apostle Paul's historic sermon on the "unknown god." President Lee reflected on Paul's mission:

"Here then was the opening of the work among the Grecian people. As Paul began to expound the doctrine, he gave us a key as to how we all could know that Jesus was the Christ. He said to the Corinthians, 'No man speaking by the Spirit of God calleth Jesus accursed: and no man can say [the Prophet Joseph Smith said that should have been translated "and no man can *know*"] that Jesus is the Lord, but by the Holy Ghost.' So we who have been baptized and received the gift of the Holy Ghost, we too can know by the witness of the Spirit that he is the Christ, to know which is to gain eternal life."

By this time several Greek members of the Church had joined the gathering, so President Lee extended his talk. His desire to live each day to the fullest was well expressed:

"As we come to positions of trust and responsibility centuries later, bearing the same message, teaching the same gospel, worshipping the same God, faced with the same opposition, we must not hesitate or slacken our zeal to project the work of the Lord. The work of the Lord never was presented with ease. It had to be brought forth out of blood and sweat and tears and sacrifice. So it may require that in our day, too, more than we know. As I read back over the history of the Presidents of the Church in our dispensation, I have become aware that all of these men went through periods of trial and testing before they came to their position in the Church. So, today, may this kind of a meeting make each one of us have a feeling of dedication."

After President Lee's powerful testimony, Elder Hinckley offered a benediction. Elder Hinckley's prayer was "so eloquent and sweeping yet so humble" that President Lee said, "We shall let that prayer become a prayer of rededication of this land."[8]

After meeting with officials of the Greek government and the Greek Orthodox Church, the Lees and Hinckleys flew to Israel. For three days they toured sacred sites and met with government officials, including Jerusalem mayor Teddy Kollek, who said a park might be developed on the Mount of Olives and that it might be possible to erect a statue commemorating Apostle Orson Hyde's dedication of the Holy Land in 1841. He promised to write President Lee on the status of the project.

As President Lee's son-in-law and biographer L. Brent Goates relates:

"There were additional fascinating visits to high officials and some beginning stops to see the sacred shrines of Jesus' ministry. In early evening they came to the Garden Tomb, where about thirty Saints who live in Israel gathered to be with the prophet. The light from a bright, September moon filtered through the olive trees, spreading a soft glow over the Garden Tomb area in Jerusalem. Ordinarily at this hour the spot would have been deserted, but on this occasion a special meeting was about to take place on this night of September 30, 1972. . . .

"President Harold B. Lee, the prophet of God, who only recently had been ordained to that calling, was now presiding at a meeting in those holy surroundings. Hymns were sung and prayers were spoken. Organizing a Jerusalem branch of the Church was an idea which came unpremeditated as inspiration of the moment. David B. Galbraith was sustained as the president of the first branch of the Church of Jesus Christ to be organized in the Holy Land in nearly two thousand years. A children's chorus sang 'I Am a Child of God.' Then, Elder Gordon B. Hinckley spoke movingly, recounting from the book of John some of the events of the death, burial, and resurrection of the Savior. President Lee's sermon was then delivered."

President Lee told the group: "Though you are few in number, you are laying the foundation of something that will be great." He further stated that the reception from various officials had been much more than the Church leaders could have hoped for.

The group sang "Now Let Us Rejoice," and Brother Brandly offered the benediction. Then Brother Galbraith was set apart before the final hymn, "God Be with You Till We Meet Again." It was a truly remarkable meeting.

But the intense pace of the trip had weakened President Lee, who had suffered from health problems for years. "These are exhausting days," he wrote. "My physical strength is at a seriously low ebb. I know something is seriously wrong. There is a severe pain in my lower back and a weariness that was emphasized by a constant effort to expel mucus. Joan insisted that I have Brother Hinckley and President Cannon administer to me." Concerning that blessing, President Lee wrote:

"The next morning, after a severe coughing spell, I expelled two clots which seemed to be blood—one, about the size of a dime, was like dried blood, and the other one was red, as a fresh clot. Immediately my shortness of breath ceased, the weariness was diminished, and the back pains began to subside, and twenty-four hours later they were entirely gone.

"I now realize I was skirting on the brink of eternity and a miracle, in this land of even greater miracles, was extended by a merciful God who obviously was prolonging my ministry for a longer time, to give to him in whose service I am all the strength of my heart, mind, and soul, to indicate in some measure my gratitude for his never-failing consideration to me and my loved ones."

President Lee was blessed to complete the trip in good health. Elder Hinckley later recalled:

"All four of us came home feeling well. I have never taken a trip for so long a period and felt better than I have on this trip. I have not had a single sick day and have felt well. We have witnessed a miracle in the restoration of the President's health. Moreover, the respite from the pressures of his office has been a wonderful relief for him. The good he has done in getting out among the people can never be estimated. They will never forget the occasions of meetings when he bore testimony, and personal interviews when they listened to him and shook hands with the Lord's chosen prophet.

"And for Marge and me it has been an incomparable experience, one we shall never forget. The unfailing kindness of President Lee and his delightful companion made traveling with them a joy and a privilege.

"We thank our Heavenly Father for his blessings. His watchful care has been over us. We have been preserved from accident and evil. His Spirit has gone before us to touch the hearts of those on whom we have called. Nature has favored us and men have respected us and honored us. We have given encouragement to a thousand missionaries, have enjoyed them, and have been enriched by their expressions of faith. We have borne testimony to the Saints in England, Greece, Israel, Italy, and Switzerland. We have walked where Jesus walked and testified of his divinity as the Son of the Living God. We have declared our knowledge of these things where Paul declared his knowledge centuries ago. We have proclaimed the prophetic calling of Joseph Smith and affirmed the prophetic calling of his successor in office, Harold B. Lee.

"This has been a journey to remember. This has been an experience to cherish."⁹

This landmark trip is an excellent illustration of a focus President Lee had throughout life—to make the most of each day, to truly make each day a masterpiece.

"HE JUST HAD TO MOVE AT TOP SPEED"

In a reminiscence that in many ways typified Harold B. Lee's entire life, his daughter Helen recalled how he did indeed seek to make the most of life:

"Daddy learned in his early years that if he was going to accomplish anything, he was going to have to move fast. And I mean that literally. His movements were always very quick, and I suppose that as he got busier and as his life became more complicated, he just had to move at top speed to get everything done—especially with a big yard to take care of. He'd come in from work, greet all of us, then upstairs he would go and change his clothes, wasting not a minute. In his old clothes, he'd start to cut the lawn before supper, while mother was still getting things on the table. It might be that he'd get a call—somebody wanted him to come and administer to him or somebody needed counsel or help. He would race back in, put on his suit again, take care of the administration or other business, come back, change his clothes again, work for a while, and then go off to an evening meeting. He wouldn't have had time to do all that if he moved at a normal pace."¹⁰

Harold B. Lee was born 28 March 1899 in Clifton, Idaho, to Samuel Lee and Louisa Bingham. Married Fern Lucinda Tanner 14 November 1923. Two children. (She died 24 September 1962.) Married Freda Joan Jensen 17 June 1963. Ordained an apostle 10 April 1941 by Heber J. Grant at age forty-two. Ordained President of the Church 7 July 1972 at age seventy-three. Died 26 December 1973 in Salt Lake City at age seventy-four.

12

"WE ARE PERMITTED SICKNESS THAT WE MIGHT LEARN PATIENCE"

Spencer W. Kimball

THE WORDS HE LIVED BY

Called as an apostle in 1943 at age forty-eight, Spencer W. Kimball served faithfully for the next forty-two years, the last twelve as Church president. His service came in the midst of a long series of health problems. Elder Kimball suffered several heart attacks in his early fifties. At one point he began planning his own funeral. He would seem to recover, then intense chest pains would return. This cycle was followed by throat problems. Over the years, each condition proved to be life-threatening, resulting in open-heart surgery and an operation to remove most of his vocal cords. On top of all this, he suffered intermittent attacks of painful boils, periodic exhaustion, skin cancer, and Bell's palsy.

Such tempering left Elder Kimball with a profound understanding of the purifying value of sickness but also with a deep empathy for anyone who endured health problems. He spoke forcefully on these subjects:

> The Lord is omnipotent, with all power to control our lives, save us pain, prevent all accidents, drive all planes and cars, feed us, protect us, save us from labor, effort, sickness, even from death. But is that what you want? Would you shield your children from effort, from disappointments, temptations, sorrows, suffering?
>
> The basic gospel law is free agency. To force us to be careful or righteous would be to nullify that fundamental law, and growth would be impossible.
>
> Should we be protected always from hardship, pain, suffering, sacrifice, or labor? Should the Lord protect the righteous? Should he immediately punish the wicked? If growth comes from fun and ease and aimless irresponsibility, then why should we ever exert ourselves to work or learn or overcome? If success is measured by the years we live, then early death is failure and tragedy. If earth life is the ultimate, how can we justify death, even in old age? If we look at mortality as a complete existence, then pain, sorrow, failure, and short life could be a calamity. But if we look upon life as an eternal thing stretching far into the pre-earth past and on into the eternal post-death future, then all happenings may be put in proper perspective.
>
> Is there not wisdom in his giving us trials that we might rise above them, responsibilities that we might achieve, work to harden our muscles, sorrows to try our souls? Are we not permitted temptations to test our strength, sickness that we might learn patience, death that we might be immortalized and glorified?
>
> . . . If mortality be the perfect state, then death would be a frustration, but the gospel teaches us there is no tragedy in death, but *only* in sin.

We know so little. *Our* judgment is so limited. We judge the Lord often with less wisdom than does our youngest child weigh our decisions.[1]

I'm grateful that my priesthood power is limited and used as the Lord sees fit to use it. I don't want to heal all the sick—for sickness sometimes is a great blessing. People become angels through sickness.

Have you ever seen someone who has been helpless for so long that he has divested himself of every envy and jealousy and ugliness in his whole life, and who has perfected his life? I have. Have you seen mothers who have struggled with, perhaps, unfortunate children for years and years, and have become saints through it? . . . I am glad that we don't have to make those decisions. No pain suffered by man or woman upon the earth will be without its compensating effects if it be suffered in resignation and if it be met with patience.[2]

Being human, we would expel from our lives, sorrow, distress, physical pain, and mental anguish and assure ourselves of continual ease and comfort. But if we closed the doors upon such, we might be evicting our greatest friends and benefactors. Suffering can make saints of people as they learn patience, long-suffering, and self-mastery. The sufferings of our Savior were part of his education.[3]

This attitude about the benefits of trials was also evident in President Kimball's discussions of prayer. If we pray insisting that the Lord grant us relief from our troubles, we may be seeking that which is not best:

Prayers are not always answered as we wish them to be. Even the Redeemer's prayer in Gethsemane was answered in the negative. He prayed that the bitter cup of sorrow, pain, and mortal life termination could pass, but the answer was a "no" answer.[4]

There may be those who pray for certain blessings without

any question in their minds as to the value of those things to them. Perhaps they are disappointed and even shaken in their faith if their prayer is not granted. Remember that our prayers are often as inconsistent and inappropriate to our Father in Heaven as are the demands of our little children upon us. What earthly parent would give to a little one a bottle of poison with which to play, even though the child might ask and demand and cry for it? Or who of you would turn a four- or six-year-old child loose with a powerful automobile, in spite of the fact that he insisted and pleaded for it? And yet we sometimes ask for just such impossible things, just such dangerous things, and the Lord in his mercy withholds them. Let us pray with the attitude always of the crucified One, "nevertheless not my will, but thine, be done." (Luke 22:42.)[5]

Do you say in your prayers: "Thy will be done"? Did you say, "Heavenly Father, if you will inspire and impress me with the right, I will do that right"? Or, did you pray, "Give me what I want or I will take it anyway"? Did you say: "Father in Heaven, I love you, I believe in you, I know you are omniscient. I am honest. I am sincerely desirous of doing right. I know you can see the end from the beginning. You can see the future. You can discern if under this situation I present, I will have peace or turmoil, happiness or sorrow, success or failure. Tell me, please, loving Heavenly Father, and I promise to do what you tell me to do." Have you prayed that way? Don't you think it might be wise? Are you courageous enough to pray that prayer? Or, are you afraid that he might not see eye to eye with you? . . . Do you want to be happy forever or for life, or do you want to satisfy only the demands of today?[6]

Our petitions are also for the sick and afflicted. The Lord will hear our sincere prayers. He may not always heal them, but he may give them peace or courage or strength to bear up.[7]

98

HE LIVED AS HE TAUGHT

"HE PRAYED WITH US AND HE BLESSED US"

In the April 1990 general conference, Elder Richard P. Lindsay of the Seventy paid tribute to President Kimball, remembering his concern for others even when he was sick himself:

"It was President Kimball who said, 'The Lord answers our prayers, but it is usually through another person that he meets our needs.' An incident in the latter part of President Kimball's ministry helped me to better understand his message and the way his own life witnessed to the truthfulness of his inspired counsel.

"As a stake president during this period, I went to a local hospital to visit a dear sister suffering with a terminal illness. More than forty years earlier, I had attended school with both this sister and her husband, who had been childhood sweethearts. But they had not been blessed with children of their own, and they had filled this void by his serving as a Scout leader—and his loving companion as the "Scout mother"—to scores of young boys over a generation.

"As I approached the hospital that day, my heart was heavy with foreboding for what lay ahead in the lives of this choice couple. For weeks this dear brother had stayed with his companion at the hospital day and night to give comfort and ease her burden and the pain of her suffering.

"As I reached the door of her hospital room that day, I met my friend emerging from his wife's room into the hallway. Unlike my earlier visits, when his countenance reflected the weight of their ordeal, this time his face was radiant and his eyes were aglow. Before I could utter a word, he said, 'You will never guess what just

WORDS TO LIVE BY

happened. As my wife and I were feeling so burdened, into our room came President Kimball'—himself a patient at the hospital, where he had recently undergone surgery. 'He prayed with us and he blessed us, and it was as though the Savior himself had come to lift our burdens.' Many other patients in that hospital, I might add, experienced a similar blessing from one who knew so much of pain and suffering."[8]

"TELL SISTER KIMBALL WE'RE GOING"

In 1976, eighty-one-year-old President Spencer W. Kimball and his wife, Camilla, traveled to the Pacific for nine area conferences. On their way to the third conference, in New Zealand, both of them became seriously ill, with headaches, coughing, nausea, and temperatures of 104. Although they had to be helped onboard the plane, they were determined to attend the conference. Spencer was facing the pressure of a television interview and a meeting with the prime minister to be held on their arrival. In addition, all conference sessions had been scheduled, and Saints in New Zealand had made plans to attend.

They slept as best they could during the flight from Western Samoa. Despite their extreme discomfort, they kept their senses of humor. As the pilot was preparing to land, Spencer found that his fever had broken. As he put on his tie he asked Camilla to brush his hair. "Which one?" she joked.

An enthusiastic crowd welcomed them, not knowing they were sick. Spencer made it through the interview and the meeting with Prime Minister Muldoon. Then his fever came on again, and he went immediately to bed.

President and Sister Kimball had been scheduled to attend a cultural program on Saturday evening, but they were still ill. President N. Eldon Tanner was with them, and Spencer requested that President Tanner attend the program in their stead. Spencer and Camilla were just hoping to make it to the Sunday sessions the next day.

About the time the program was scheduled to start, however, Spencer suddenly woke. He turned to Dr. Russell Nelson, who had accompanied him and Camilla, and asked what time the program was scheduled to start.

"At seven o'clock, President Kimball."

"What time is it now?"

"It is almost seven."

Spencer found that his fever had broken. "Tell Sister Kimball we're going," he said.

Camilla also felt well enough to go, and they rushed to the stadium. President Tanner had already explained to the huge crowd that President and Sister Kimball were too ill to be there. But in the opening prayer a young New Zealander had humbly requested of the Lord, "We three thousand New Zealand youth have gathered here prepared to sing and to dance for thy prophet. Wilt thou heal him and deliver him here."

"As the prayer ended, the car carrying Spencer and Camilla entered and the stadium erupted in a spontaneous, deafening shout at the answer to their prayer."[9]

Once again, President Kimball had faced trial and difficulty—and had emerged victorious.

"COMFORTING OTHERS LESS ILL THAN HE"

After President Kimball's death at age ninety in 1985, Elder Neal A. Maxwell offered a moving tribute:

"These and so many other traits are indelibly inscribed in our hearts and minds as we ponder the life of President Kimball. Next to the Savior's preeminent gospel, which he preached so tirelessly and earnestly, President Kimball placed the example of his own life. This man was a message himself! Whereas the presiding role of most other latter-day prophets had been expected by Church members, the coming of President Spencer W. Kimball to the presidency of the Church was not generally anticipated. But how quickly the full mantle fell upon him! . . .

"In pondering proposed surgery, there was an episode in 1972 which is both inspiring and sobering. Elder (then Dr.) Russell M. Nelson described that dramatic moment:

"'In the month of March, I joined with President Kimball as he assembled his wife and the First Presidency. President Kimball said, "I am an old man. I am ready to die. It is time for a younger man to come to the Quorum and do the work I can no longer do." President Lee interrupted and pounded his fist on the desk and said, "Spencer, you have been called not to die but to live." President Kimball then humbly and submissively announced, "In that case, I will have the operation." Sister Kimball wept. The decision had been made.' (From a devotional speech at Weber State College, 10 Nov. 1978.)

"Looking back, it is difficult to imagine this dispensation without the presidency of Spencer W. Kimball. How grateful we should all be that another prophet, President Harold B. Lee, counseled President Kimball so directly and so lovingly with regard to proceeding with that heart surgery. Obedient as prophets are with each other, President Kimball followed the counsel of his senior Apostle. As a result, millions have been blessed by the ministry of this man who had fully expected to wear himself out as a member of the Council of the Twelve. . . .

"Even as he was being further tutored by the Lord in visible and touching demonstrations of the principle 'all these things shall give thee experience and shall be for thy good,' the rest of us were being tutored indirectly at the same time. We were not, in fact, abstract observers, because of our love for President Kimball. We were, in a sense, coparticipants in his personal drama, which was laden with lessons as it unfolded before our very eyes. . . .

"Through this man, the Lord taught us yet a final lesson as President Kimball struggled in his remaining days after multiple surgery. This time he did not experience the full resilience which followed previous illnesses. Yet, again, there was that same flintlike determination to proceed about his duties as best he could and endure well to the end—at the same time comforting others less ill than he.

"In his final days, this prophet who had always responded with a ringing, 'I'll go where you want me to go, dear Lord,' in like manner responded obediently and touchingly when the response to the final requirement evoked, 'I'll stay where you want me to stay, dear Lord.' . . .

"His many visits to the sick in homes and hospitals were legendary. One hospital patient, who himself had been through the trauma of open heart surgery, received a surprise visit from President Kimball. This dear brother had been under the influence of tobacco but reported, 'Although I had cut way down at that time, I've never touched another cigarette since I held the hand of the prophet!'"[10]

Spencer W. Kimball was born 28 March 1895 in Salt Lake City to Andrew Kimball and Olive Woolley. Married Camilla Eyring 16 November 1917. Four children. Ordained an apostle 7 October 1943 at age forty-eight by Heber J. Grant. Ordained President of the Church 30 December 1973 at age seventy-eight. Died 5 November 1985 in Salt Lake City at age ninety.

13

"DO THE RIGHT THING AND LET THE CHIPS FALL WHERE THEY WILL"

Ezra Taft Benson

THE WORDS HE LIVED BY

When a newspaper reporter asked Ezra Taft Benson, then Secretary of Agriculture, his secret for staying calm in the midst of pressure and controversy, Ezra replied: "It's easy to keep calm if you have inner security and peace of mind. . . . I try to do the thing I believe to be right and let the chips fall where they will."[1]

Both in his teachings and in his life, President Benson continually emphasized doing the right thing and letting the consequences follow:

The gospel of Jesus Christ has always been essentially a plan for living more abundantly. To do so requires righteous, worthwhile effort and application. If we are to pattern our lives in accordance with the divine example set for us by the Savior, we must attain to that stature by releasing and developing our capacities to the fullest through devoted service. Only in this way may we become worthy examples of the kingdom of God on earth and merit consideration for membership in the kingdom of God in heaven.[2]

President Benson stressed that by doing the right thing, we set a good example for others:

The proper example is all-important. Let us be what we profess to be. There is no satisfactory substitute. Who was it said, "What you are rings so loud in my ears I cannot hear what you say"? It was said of one of the great Chinese philosophers and teachers that he did not have to teach, all he had to do was to be.[3]

We do stand as witnesses before God "at all times and in all things, and in all places" by our actions (see Mosiah 18:9). When our actions are honorable, we bring credit to His Church and kingdom; when they are not, it reflects on the entire Church.[4]

Doing the right thing, President Benson taught, involves being more obedient in all areas of our lives:

We must stand as a leaven among the nations, true to the principles of righteousness. We need to be humble. We need to be grateful. We need as families to kneel in family prayer, night and morning. Just a few words added to the blessing on the food, as is becoming the custom in some parts, is not enough. We need to get onto our knees in prayer and gratitude as Alma admonished (Alma 34:17–27). We need the spirit of reverence in our houses of worship. We need to keep the Sabbath day holy. We need to close our businesses on Sunday and as Latter-day Saints refrain from making purchases on the Sabbath. We need to refrain from going to moving pictures on the Sabbath, and if we are operating show houses, we should close them on Sunday. We should not seek pleasure in any form on the Sabbath day. We should stand firm in opposition to Sunday baseball and other amusements regardless of what much of the Christian world may do. We should oppose gambling in all of its forms, including the parimutuel betting at horse races. We should refrain from card playing, against which we have been counseled by the leaders of the Church. We should stand united in opposition to the wider distribution of alcohol and other things declared by the Lord to be harmful.[5]

President Benson often spoke of *standards*, and of our need to stand firm and true to those standards, uncompromising, unwavering, regardless of what the world may do:

> We do not compromise principle. We do not surrender our standards regardless of current trends or pressures. As a Church, our allegiance to truth is unwavering.[6]
>
> Hold fast to the iron rod (1 Nephi 11:25), that we may be true to the faith, that we may maintain the standards which the Lord has set in His Church, that we might follow a course that is safe so that we may be exalted.[7]
>
> Never has the Church had the opportunity and the challenge which it faces today. Now is the time for us to arise and shine as a people (D&C 115:5), to put on our beautiful garments (2 Nephi 8:24), to demonstrate to the world the fruits of the gospel, and to proclaim the standards which the Lord has revealed for the blessings of His children.[8]
>
> Remember, . . . you will never have an occasion to be embarrassed—among people of character, people who count, real men and women—because you live according to the standards, the teachings, and ideals of the Church.[9]

106

HE LIVED AS HE TAUGHT

HOLDING TO PRINCIPLE AS SECRETARY OF AGRICULTURE

Fifty-three-year-old Ezra Taft Benson had served in the Quorum of the Twelve for nine years when he received an unexpected phone call from Utah Senator Arthur V. Watkins. The date was 20 November 1952. The senator informed him that newly elected president Dwight D. Eisenhower[10] was considering the possibility of asking Elder Benson to serve as Secretary of Agriculture.

"If you are asked," said Watkins, "will you be available to accept the position?"

"Only President McKay can answer that question," replied Ezra.

The next morning Ezra encountered David O. McKay, who had been sustained as Church president a year and a half earlier (after serving in the Quorum of the Twelve Apostles for forty-five years), in the Church Administration Building parking lot. President McKay had also received a phone call concerning Ezra's availability for the cabinet post.

"My mind is clear in the matter," said President McKay. "If the opportunity comes in the proper spirit, I think you should accept."

"I can't believe it will come," said Elder Benson, shaking his head. "If it were Dewey asking, it would be different. But I've never even *seen* Eisenhower, much less met him."

The next day, however, a request came directly from "Ike," supreme commander of the Allied forces during World War II: could Ezra meet with him in New York City in two days? Yes, replied Ezra, who immediately called President McKay. With approval from the senior apostle, Ezra left for New York City, fasting and praying (and the rest of the family doing likewise) that he would make the right decision.

Although he assumed he would be one of several candidates for the post, Ezra found on his arrival at Eisenhower's headquarters at the Hotel Commodore that he was the only candidate. Of his meeting with the general, he later wrote: "I saw a powerfully built person, a little under six feet, with a smile fresh and warm as a sunny summer's day. . . . I liked him immediately."

Eisenhower didn't beat around the bush. "Will you accept an appointment as Secretary of Agriculture?" he asked.

Not answering the question, Ezra confessed that he had supported Robert Taft, not Ike, for the Republican nomination. Further, he said, he wasn't sure that he favored a military man serving in the White House. In addition, someone from the Midwest might enjoy more popular support for the post. Lastly, should an ecclesiastical leader serve in the United States cabinet?

"Surely," countered the president-elect, "you know we have the great responsibility to restore the confidence of our people in their own government, and that means we've got to deal with spiritual matters."

Certain that this request had met President McKay's condition of coming "in the proper spirit," Elder Benson accepted. Twenty minutes later Eisenhower announced the appointment to the press. In a phone call to his wife, Flora, moments after that, Ezra said, "I feel more like praying than anything else."

This attitude served him well in the turbulent years that followed. The USDA (United States Department of Agriculture) was in a controversial, precarious position because of price supports instituted during World War II. To encourage a high level of farm production, the government had guaranteed farmers an artificially high price for their products. In the years following the war, demand for farm products had fallen but production had risen—causing even more of a gap between the market value and the government guarantee. As a result, government warehouses were filling up with commodities, and farmers were relying more and more on federal subsidies.

Rejecting the policies of his predecessor, Secretary Benson declared that "any country which pursues policies that cause the self-reliance, initiative, and freedom of its people to drain slowly away is a country in danger." He soon announced his view that rigid price supports "should be used only to protect the farmer against disaster and to stabilize the volatile commodities market—not to guarantee the farmer a living. He would support flexible price supports based on market performance, but not rigid supports. He expressed his belief that freedom was more precious than life itself, and that no person who depends upon the state for sustenance is free."

Many individual farmers supported Ezra's policies. In fact, his mail always ran heavily in his favor. Some in Congress were passionately opposed, however, and they criticized him mercilessly. "Benson," remarked Eugene McCarthy, senator from Minnesota, "is like a man standing on the bank of the river telling a drowning man that all he needs to do is take a deep breath of air."

But Secretary Benson did much more than simply talk. He crisscrossed the country, meeting with groups and with individual farmers to understand their plight. Discovering that milk was not available on airline flights, he wrote every airline president and urged them to make milk a regular menu item. He encouraged vending machine owners and operators throughout the United States to carry milk. He arranged for comedian Bob Hope to join him in promoting the American Dairyman's Association. "There may be an organization with more branch offices, but there are none that have more outlets," joked Hope.

An editorial in the *Chicago Sun-Times* stated that Eisenhower's "program makes a lot of sense to us, and we urge Congress to take Ike's advice and give it early approval."

But some groups were extremely hostile, picketing or even throwing eggs. Ezra stood firm by his principles, sometimes winning over angry crowds. When he spoke in Mississippi, that state's Senator Eastland, who had earlier been critical of Ezra, introduced him by saying, "My friends, today you're going to hear something you won't like, but it will be good for you because it's the truth." Such experiences confirmed a promise given in a blessing by President McKay: "We bless you, therefore, dear Brother Ezra, that when questions of right and wrong come before the men with whom you are deliberating, you may see clearly what is right, and knowing it, that you may have courage to stand by that which is right and proper."

Ezra's strongest support came from his wife, Flora. One newspaper stated: "Although Flora Benson is extremely retiring in public, in private she is considered to be the pivot on which the family moves. . . . Friends of the family agree that she acts as the leavening influence on her husband. Said a friend, 'Every once in a while, when it's needed, . . . she says, "Now, look here, T!" and that seems to do the trick.'"

The debate raged on, with many predicting defeat for the administration. An influential newsletter stated that "things are looking bad for Benson and company on Capital Hill—to put it mildly. Their farm program now stands less chance than ever for approval."

Appearing on television, President Eisenhower appealed to the country: "Many have told me that it would not be good politics to attempt solution of the farm problem during an election year. The sensible thing to do, I have been told . . . was to close my eyes to the damage the present farm program does to our farmers. . . . In this matter I am completely unmoved by arguments as to what constitutes good or winning politics. . . . Though I have not been in this political business very long, I know that what is right for America is politically right."

Despite Eisenhower's speech, the House Agriculture Committee quickly voted to raise price supports on dairy products, making Ezra more determined than ever to take his case to the people. Against his staff's wishes, he spoke to the National Farmers' Union in Denver. The group had voiced strong opposition to administration policies; Eisenhower called them a "bunch of rebels." After Ezra's powerful speech, however, the farmers gave him a standing ovation and gathered around to shake his hand.

In August of 1954, Eisenhower's Agricultural Act went to the Senate. Up to the last minute, Secretary Benson lobbied senators, explaining his program in detail. The Benson family waited anxiously, with Reed sending his father regular reports from the gallery. Finally the vote came, shocking many critics around the country: the Senate passed flexible price-support legislation by a vote of 49 to 44.

One headline proclaimed: *Foolish Ezra, They Said of Mr. Benson—But He Beat the Farm Bloc.*

"They . . . called [Ezra Taft Benson] stupid," wrote Scripps-Howard columnist Howard Lucey, "and denounced him as the worst Secretary of Agriculture in history and demanded that President Eisenhower fire him. But Ezra Taft Benson stood his ground and took the pounding. Today he has emerged as hero of the biggest legislative victory the Eisenhower administration has had."

Collier's magazine ran a similar story: "It would have been easier for the Secretary . . . if he had been willing to let the rigid 90 per cent of parity support remain operative. . . . But the issue as Secretary Benson saw it was not wholly or even mainly political. It was first economic, and ultimately moral."[11]

"Mothers Should Be Full-time Mothers"

In the mid-1980s—more than thirty years after gaining national respect for his concern with principle—Ezra Taft Benson once again spoke out on a controversial topic. In July 1986, eight months after being sustained as President of the Church, President Benson spoke at the Provo Freedom Festival. As he discussed the Founding Fathers and the United States Constitution, he also noted that mothers had a primary responsibility to their children. This part of his address, however, was not mentioned in news stories covering his speech. President Benson wrote in his journal: "I don't know whether it was . . . not wanting to stir up controversy that the statement which I made that mothers should be full-time mothers in the home was not mentioned. I feel very deeply regarding this question, and expect to speak on it later."

President Benson did speak out six months later in a Church-wide fireside, advising parents not to delay having children. He further admonished fathers to provide for their families so that their wives would not be forced to work. "The Lord clearly defined the roles of mothers and fathers in providing for and rearing a righteous posterity," he said. "In the beginning, Adam—not Eve—was instructed to earn the bread by the sweat of his brow. Contrary to conventional wisdom, a mother's calling is in the home, not the marketplace. . . . Mothers, this kind of heavenly, motherly teaching takes time—lots of time. It cannot be done effectively part time. It must be done all the time in order to save and exalt your children."

Such statements came at a time when the role of women was being hotly debated throughout the country. Just a few years earlier, the proposed Equal Rights Amendment had created deep divisions. Not surprisingly, President Benson's speech drew both strong support and bitter argument. Many women wrote to thank him for his strong stand, but there were also some, both in and out of the Church, who objected to his views.

Once again, Ezra Taft Benson did what he believed was right, letting the chips fall where they would. Rather than apologizing for his remarks, he had his address reprinted in pamphlet form so that it could be distributed throughout the Church by way of home teachers. And while attention focused on President Benson, some of his comments deemed controversial were actually quotes from his predecessor, President Kimball. "Too many mothers work away from home to furnish sweaters and music lessons and trips and fun for their children," President Kimball had said. "Too many women spend their time in socializing, in politicking, in public services when they should be home to teach and train and receive and love their children into security."

National radio commentator Paul Harvey noted that "the President of the Mormon Church, Ezra Taft Benson, says mothers should stay home and care for their children." Harvey accurately added that "President Benson's three predecessors have all said the same thing: that mothers should stay home and care for their children."

Even those who disagreed with President Benson's views had to agree that he was a man of deep integrity, a man who said in plain language what he believed and then stuck to it. In his characteristic way, President Benson had once again taken a bold, uncompromising stand on principle. Just as he had three decades earlier, he weathered the storm of controversy and persuaded many to rethink their assumptions.[12]

Ezra Taft Benson was born 4 August 1899 in Whitney, Idaho, to George Taft Benson and Sarah Dunkley. Married Flora Smith Amussen 10 September 1926. Six children. Ordained an apostle 7 October 1943 at age forty-four by Heber J. Grant. (Ordained the same day but immediately after Spencer W. Kimball.) Ordained President of the Church 10 November 1985 at age eighty-six. Died 30 May 1994 in Salt Lake City at age ninety-four.

14

"THE TOUCHSTONE OF COMPASSION IS A MEASURE OF OUR DISCIPLESHIP"

THE WORDS HE LIVED BY

In 1990, the United States Court of Appeals for the Ninth Circuit in California honored eighty-three-year-old Howard W. Hunter (then president of the Quorum of the Twelve) for his fifty years as a member of the California State Bar. Prominent Los Angeles attorney John S. Welch noted that President Hunter "epitomizes the practice of law in the classic style: honor, ethical conduct, courtesy, gentility, the art of making the adversarial system work while sticking to the rules, and . . . integrity."[1]

Indeed, such words as *courtesy* and *gentility* captured the essence of Howard W. Hunter, who often proclaimed the primacy of compassion:

The touchstone of compassion is a measure of our disciple-ship; it is a measure of our love for God and for one another. Will we leave a mark of pure gold or, like the priest and the Levite, will we pass by on the other side?[2]

A touchstone, he explained, was used in ancient times to test the purity of gold. The touchstone was "a smooth, black, siliceous stone. . . . When rubbed across the touchstone, the gold produced a streak or mark on its surface. The goldsmith matched this mark to a color on his chart of graded colors. The mark was redder as the amount of copper or alloy increased or yellower as the percentage of gold increased. This process showed quite accurately the purity of the gold."

Sometimes the goldsmith subjected the gold to an additional, more accurate test, "using a process that involved fire."

I suggest to you that the Lord has prepared a touchstone for you and me, an outward measurement of inward discipleship that marks our faithfulness and will survive the fires yet to come.

He will measure our devotion to him by how we love and serve our fellowmen. What kind of mark are we leaving on the Lord's touchstone? Are we truly good neighbors? Does the test show us to be 24-karat gold, or can the trace of fool's gold be detected?[3]

In this time of periodic war and strife in the Middle East, President Hunter's teachings of compassion seem particularly applicable:

It should be manifestly evident to members of the Church that our Father loves all of his children. He desires all of them to embrace the gospel and come unto him. Only those are favored who obey him and keep his commandments.

As members of the Lord's church, we need to lift our vision beyond personal prejudices. We need to discover the supreme truth that indeed our Father is no respecter of persons. Sometimes we unduly offend brothers and sisters of other nations by assigning exclusiveness to one nationality of people over another. . . .

We have members of the Church in the Muslim world. These are wonderful Saints, good members of the Church. They live in Iran, Egypt, Lebanon, Saudi Arabia, and other countries. Sometimes they are offended by members of the Church who give the impression that we favor only the aims of the Jews. The Church has an interest in all of Abraham's descendants, and we should remember that the history of the Arabs goes back to Abraham through his son Ishmael.

Imagine a father with many sons, each having different temperaments, aptitudes, and spiritual traits. Does he love one son less than another? Perhaps the son who is least spiritually inclined has the father's attention, prayers, and pleadings more than the others. Does that mean he loves the others less? Do you imagine our Heavenly Father loving one nationality of his offspring more exclusively than others? As members of the Church, we need to be reminded of Nephi's challenging question: "Know ye not that there are more nations than one?" (2 Nephi 29:7).[4]

HE LIVED AS HE TAUGHT

"ALL MANKIND WERE HIS FRIENDS"

Speaking at President Hunter's funeral, Elder Jon M. Huntsman remembered his Christlike life:

"Such was the warm and gracious friendship of our beloved prophet and President, Howard William Hunter. He was a loyal, devoted, and loving friend to so many. To his neighbors, his home was always open, and his exuberance and warm affection attracted many. All the traits embodied by our Lord and Savior, Jesus Christ, were beautifully characterized in President Hunter's remarkable and selfless life. All mankind were his friends.

"To those friends who may have transgressed or been offended, he welcomed them back to the fold.

"To those friends who were hurt and struggling and afraid, he said, 'Let us stand with you and dry your tears' (*Ensign*, Nov. 1994, p. 8).

"To many of his neighbors' sons and daughters who mowed his lawn or shoveled snow from his sidewalk, he would always call with a gracious expression of appreciation and surprise.

"The President, with his profound knowledge and a background of such diverse talents, would often meet with those not of our faith—and he uplifted them. 'Love all men,' the Savior said, and this gentle and kind prophet of God did just that. No one ever felt uncomfortable in his presence. He was our friend. . . .

"Thank you, dear President, for permitting us to learn from you humility and graciousness. How often you quietly listened while others were telling you something you already knew—and yet you thanked them, complimented them, and made them feel so very important. You were such a kind and thoughtful listener. You possessed a remarkable and quick sense of humor, particularly during times of physical or emotional stress or illness. It would always manifest itself in such delightful ways. To those who helped you to the podium, you would often say, 'Brethren, I hope next time you won't need my help.' To those helping you to your seat afterwards, you would quietly whisper, 'Just drop me anyplace.'

"Thank you, dear President, for reminding us of the sacred nature of the holy sacrament, when only the Sunday before your passing you suggested to those few present how joyous it would be to participate therein. Perhaps you knew far more than us that this occasion would represent your last Sabbath day in mortality. With humility and great honor, your friends knelt and blessed and passed the sacrament. Your remarks immediately thereafter were memorable. You stated, 'Thank you, dear brethren. What a great honor and privilege to partake of the Lord's sacrament.' . . .

"Thank you, dear President, for loving the Savior so deeply. You spent your life learning of him and speaking of him. He was your best friend. You helped us become closer to our elder Brother. You understood so well Christ's atonement and the importance of the Resurrection. You became much like him. You gave hope to all of us who stumble as you gently lifted us and offered the light and the way. You provided a vital glimpse of your 'sure knowledge' when near the end you sweetly stated, 'Let's look for each other on the other side.'

"Good-bye for now, dear prophet and friend. Your Christlike qualities and goodness will be greatly missed. You are our hero. We love you forever and ever."[5]

A Tribute from Elder Jeffrey R. Holland

When he was called as an apostle in June of 1994, Elder Jeffrey R. Holland experienced the compassion of Howard W. Hunter first-hand, even though President Hunter was suffering serious health problems at the time—and would pass away nine months later. Elder Holland recalled:

"One divine manifestation I have seen is of the prophetic calling of President Howard W. Hunter, whom we had the privilege of sustaining this morning in solemn assembly. Because of the unexpected call which came to me in the first weeks of his prophetic ministry, I have had something of a unique vantage point from which to observe the miracle of his renewal, the profound evidence of God's hand upon this chosen leader.

"In a rapid sequence of events that Thursday morning, President Hunter interviewed me at length, extended to me my call, formally introduced me to the First Presidency and the Twelve gathered in their temple meeting, gave me my apostolic charge and outline of duties, ordained me an Apostle, set me apart as a member of the Quorum of the Twelve, added a magnificent and beautiful personal blessing of considerable length, then went on to conduct the sacred business of that first of my temple meetings, lasting another two or three hours!

"President Hunter did all of that personally. And through it all he was strong and fixed and powerful. Indeed, it seemed to me he got stronger and more powerful as the day progressed. I count it one of the greatest privileges of my life just to have observed the Lord's anointed engaged in such a manner. . . .

"Yes, I testify that God has worked his will on Howard William Hunter. He has touched his lips and spread the prophetic mantle of ordained leadership upon his shoulders. President Hunter is a miracle—one who has been fashioned, molded, refined, and sustained for the service he now renders. He is a most remarkable blend of velvet and steel. Like every prophet before him—including Joseph Smith, Jr.—and every prophet who will succeed him, President Hunter was called and foreordained in the grand councils of heaven before this world was. I bear solemn witness of that fact and the principle of Church governance it teaches. And age? Age has nothing to do with it. Whether an incomparable fourteen-year-old in 1820 or an invincible eighty-six-year-old in 1994, it is obvious that the number of birthdays doesn't count, that 'time . . . is measured [only] unto men' (Alma 40:8). President Hunter, we all bask in the glow of those candles on your cake and look forward to lighting yet another one in six weeks' time."[6]

Fellowshipping the Russian Saints

When President and Sister Hunter visited Russia in 1992, President Gary Browning of the Russia Moscow Mission recalled the graciousness and love manifested by President Hunter at a meeting in Moscow, yet another manifestation of the inherent compassion of this wonderful prophet:

"In September Elder and Sister Howard W. Hunter visited Moscow and spoke to five hundred gathered at a Sunday service. The meeting went well and was fulfilling from the standpoint of spiritual nourishment. But what I will recall occurred after the meeting when hundreds quietly filed past Elder Hunter and shook his hand. No one took much of his time, but all wished him good health and joy. I stood next to Elder Hunter, translating for him, and had the unforgettable experience of looking into our members' eyes as they spoke to Elder Hunter. I wish I could convey the nonverbal expressions of faith, purity, and human warmth that flowed from their smiles and gaze. To think that a few months ago most of them were just learning of the gospel and Church, and that a few years ago they would have had great difficulty professing any religious conviction. Now they radiated gratitude and love for an apostle and prophet that was both inspiring and confirming."[7]

Howard W. Hunter was born 14 November 1907 in Boise, Idaho, to John William Hunter and Nellie Marie Rasmussen. Married Clara May (Claire) Jeffs 10 June 1931. Three children. (She died 9 October 1983.) Married Inis Bernice Egan 12 April 1990. Ordained an apostle 15 October 1959 at age fifty-one by David O. McKay. Ordained President of the Church 5 June 1994 at age eighty-six. Died 3 March 1995 in Salt Lake City at age eighty-seven.

15

"ONE OF THE GREATEST VALUES IS THE VIRTUE OF HONEST WORK"

THE WORDS HE LIVED BY

President Gordon B. Hinckley has become well known among the Saints for his love of hard work. From his building his own home as a young husband to his demanding travel schedule during the 1980s and 1990s, President Hinckley has shown the value of work by example.

As President Thomas S. Monson has noted, President Hinckley combines this work ethic with the ability to concentrate on the task at hand: "President Hinckley can juggle a lot of balls in the air at the same time. He can go from a meeting where the item is welfare to another where the topic is auditing and then to another where proselyting is being discussed, and be able to instantly switch gears and give undivided attention to that subject."[1]

Fittingly, President Hinckley has emphasized this principle in his sermons:

There is no substitute for [work]. Jehovah established the law when He declared, "In the sweat of thy face shalt thou eat bread." (Genesis 3:19.) . . .

Some years ago a Boeing 707 jet took off from Idlewild airport. It rose into the sky and then suddenly plunged into the Jamaica mud, taking eighty-nine people to their deaths. The months of investigation that followed brought the conclusion that a workman in a New Jersey subcontractor's plant had carelessly handled a wire in putting together a servo mechanism that was assembled into the plane in the Boeing plant in Seattle. This all-important little wire, smaller than a pencil, connected with evident neglect, had caused a short circuit, wresting the plane from the control of the pilot and plunging it into the mud, with a fearsome loss of life and property.

Shoddy workmanship, lack of pride in labor, the repeated coffee breaks that rob employers of the time of those they hire are all characteristic of a flagrant dishonesty and a warped sense of obligation that afflicts so many of our people.

I should like to say to you tonight that one of the greatest values . . . is the virtue of honest work. Knowledge without labor is profitless. Knowledge with labor is genius."[2]

I believe in the gospel of work. There is no substitute under the heavens for productive labor. It is the process by which dreams become reality. It is the process by which idle visions become dynamic achievements. We are all inherently lazy. We would rather play than work. We would rather loaf than work. A little play and a little loafing are good—that is one of the reasons you are here. But it is work that spells the difference in the life of a man or woman. It is stretching our minds and utilizing the skills of our hands that lifts us from the stagnation of mediocrity.[3]

HE LIVED AS HE TAUGHT

THE WORK ETHIC OF A NEWLY RETURNED MISSIONARY

From 1933 to 1935, young Gordon B. Hinckley served in the European Mission under mission president and apostle Joseph F. Merrill, who had been called into the Quorum of the Twelve in 1931. Of President Merrill, Lawrence R. Flake has written:

"The London office staff of the European Mission may have thought their new mission president somewhat austere. He lived in a fourth-floor apartment with no elevator, ate a modest diet with little meat or rich foods, exercised in the mornings, walked each evening, and shaved with cold water. He also counseled them to turn the lights out when leaving a room. But these frugal and healthful habits were only the exterior of Brother Joseph F. Merrill, a man careful with Church funds but generous with his own means. The sign on the door, 'European Mission,' gave occasional passersby the idea that it was a soup kitchen, and destitute wanderers sometimes rang the bell. President Merrill never let them go away hungry. One of his missionaries recalled seeing a poorly clad young man leaving, wearing one of the mission president's own coats. . . .

"[Joseph] worked as a water boy to a railroad construction gang when he was only eleven, and at the age of thirteen he was driving team for construction crews, a job usually filled by a grown man. . . . He never ceased to work, and he often said he had never missed a day's work because of illness. At the Church Office Building he was known for keeping long hours, arriving habitually at seven-thirty in the morning, and not leaving until the same hour in the evening."[4]

This enthusiasm for fruitful labor was not lost on Elder

Hinckley. When he returned home in the summer of 1935, he went right to work on a task requested by President Merrill: to meet with the First Presidency and discuss the dearth of good Church literature in the mission field and suggest possible solutions, including professionally produced lectures and filmstrips. On 21 August 1935, Gordon, then twenty-five years old, wrote to President Merrill:

"At last I have seen the First Presidency. After trying for more than two weeks, I was given an appointment for last Tuesday, day before yesterday. Presidents Grant and McKay were there, Joseph Anderson took down in shorthand my report, and before I had finished the Presiding Bishopric came in and heard of our troubles.

"I told them plainly of what was being done, and of the difficulty we had in securing the things we desired. I warmed up on the illustrated lectures. Brother McKay expressed himself as being heartily in favor of the thing. The President was noncommittal. They have been terribly busy since they returned from the East; my time was up at 10 o'clock and I was obliged to leave at five minutes past ten. . . .

"You will recall that we sent . . . copies of two lectures. But it appears they are now lost. In going from the hands of one committeeman to another they have doubtless been placed at the bottom of a big pile of papers where they now lie—Peace to their bones. . . . I read [a sixty-page script] and had to [reply] in my most tactful manner that I did not think it suitable for our needs. [I was told] that I should take it and rebuild it for our needs. And so . . . I am taking [the] material and trying to wrench from the mass at least one lecture that will interest people in the Book of Mormon. Wow! what a task. I've been at it for a week now, and the thing is so unwieldy that I haven't completed it yet. But I hope to get it out of the way by tonight."[5]

Responding to a previous letter from Gordon, President Merrill wrote on August 23: "Yes, any film strip or set of pictures should be accompanied by a carefully prepared lecture. The pictures alone without the lecture would lack very much of their effectiveness. . . .

"You are finding the situation there as I think I indicated a number of times. The brethren are sympathetic but they are extremely busy. . . . Of course we are very grateful for the sympathy and hope that they will put you on the job at a reasonable salary to carry forward our project. What we recently said in 3 or 4 letters written to various members of the Council of Twelve might be very helpful in this direction."[6]

Of the meeting with young Gordon B. Hinckley, President Heber J. Grant noted, "At 9:30 met Gordon B. Hinckley . . . who has been on a mission in Great Britain, and made suggestions regarding getting articles in the British Press. He was very successful while laboring in the British Mission in getting a great deal of fine matter in the London and other papers and magazines."[7]

In his letter to President Merrill, Gordon had mentioned his possible interest in returning to school (he had already received a bachelor's degree in English from the University of Utah). However, two days after his meeting with the First Presidency, Gordon received a call from David O. McKay, then second counselor in the First Presidency to Heber J. Grant.

"Brother Hinckley," he said, "we discussed in the meeting of the Presidency and the Twelve yesterday what we talked about during your interview with us. And we have organized a committee consisting of six members of the Twelve, with Elder Stephen L Richards as chairman, to address the needs you outlined. We would like to invite you to come and work with that committee."[8]

By accepting a $65-a-month position as executive secretary of the newly formed Church Radio, Publicity, and Mission Literature Committee, Gordon B. Hinckley began his long career of historic

Church service. By 1939 he was supervising production of a Church exhibit at the San Francisco World's Fair. He was sustained as an Assistant to the Twelve in 1958 and as an apostle in 1961. When he was ordained President of the Church on 12 March 1995, he remembered his hard-working mentors Joseph F. Merrill and Heber J. Grant:

"It will be sixty years ago in July that I first came into this room as a newly returned missionary to meet with the First Presidency at the request of my mission president, Elder Joseph F. Merrill of the Council of the Twelve. It is difficult to realize what has happened since then. To think that I now sit where President Heber J. Grant sat at that time. He was a giant of a man whom I loved."[9]

"PRESIDENT HINCKLEY IS TIRELESS"

During his tenure as President of the Church, President Hinckley has continued to emphasize, in his personal service, the highest level of commitment to hard work. He was sustained the fifteenth Church president on 12 March 1995 and immediately launched into a rigorous schedule. He traveled to numerous locations in the United States, and then made back-to-back trips to Asia and Europe. On one occasion he conducted an interview on an East coast radio station and was introduced as the first "sitting President of the Church to visit New England since President Joseph F. Smith." President Hinckley responded with characteristic wit—but also with an indication of his intention to move forward vigorously: "I am not a sitting President, I am a running President."[10]

"President Hinckley is tireless," President Boyd K. Packer has said. "He's got all of us running to keep up with him."[11] And after a trip to Asia with President Hinckley, Elder Joseph B. Wirthlin remarked, "The last couple of weeks have been similar to running a marathon."[12]

On a trip to England, "almost every day he and Sister Hinckley traveled by car to a new city, often more than a hundred miles away, and met with missionaries, inspected property, gave media interviews, and held special firesides for the members. In all he delivered fourteen addresses to nearly eight thousand Saints during the whirlwind trip, which revealed just how much stamina the eighty-five-year-old Church President had. 'He is only happy when he is getting things done,' Sister Hinckley said afterward. 'I just try to keep up with him, and that isn't easy. He is a very young eighty-five.'"[13]

President Hinckley was once asked how he maintained his incredible pace. He answered with his usual humor: "I go to bed every night and make sure I get up the next morning. I just keep going." Then he added, "You get your lift from the people. They give me the energy to keep going. I love being among the Saints."[14]

Gordon B. Hinckley was born 23 June 1910 in Salt Lake City to Bryant S. Hinckley and Ada Bitner. Married Marjorie Pay 29 April 1937. Five children. Sustained an Assistant to the Twelve 6 April 1958. Ordained an apostle 5 October 1961 at age fifty-one by David O. McKay. Ordained President of the Church 12 March 1995 at age eighty-four.

CHRONOLOGY

1 June 1801	Birth of Brigham Young, Whitingham, Vermont
1804–06	Lewis and Clark Expedition
23 December 1805	Birth of Joseph Smith, Sharon, Vermont
1 March 1807	Birth of Wilford Woodruff, Farmington, Connecticut
1 November 1808	Birth of John Taylor, Milnthorpe, England
3 April 1814	Birth of Lorenzo Snow, Mantua, Ohio
Spring 1820	First Vision
22 September 1827	Joseph Smith receives plates from Moroni
6 April 1830	Organization of the Church; Joseph Smith sustained as First Elder
27 March 1836	Dedication of the Kirtland Temple
20 June 1837	Victoria becomes Queen of Great Britain
13 November 1838	Birth of Joseph F. Smith, Far West, Missouri
27 June 1844	Joseph and Hyrum murdered, Carthage, Illinois
22–24 July 1847	First pioneer company reaches the Great Salt Lake Valley
5 December 1847	Brigham Young becomes second President of the Church
24 January 1848	Gold discovered at Sutter's Mill, California
Fall 1856	More than 200 members of the Willie and Martin handcart companies perish on the trail
22 November 1856	Birth of Heber J. Grant, Salt Lake City

13 April 1861	U.S. Civil War begins
9 April 1865	U.S. Civil War ends
15 April 1865	Abraham Lincoln assassinated
4 April 1870	Birth of George Albert Smith, Salt Lake City
8 September 1873	Birth of David O. McKay, Huntsville, Utah
19 July 1876	Birth of Joseph Fielding Smith, Salt Lake City
29 August 1877	Death of Brigham Young, Salt Lake City
25 August 1878	Primary program is organized
21 October 1879	Thomas Edison successfully tests an electric light bulb
10 October 1880	John Taylor becomes third President of the Church
25 July 1887	Death of John Taylor, Kaysville, Utah
7 April 1889	Wilford Woodruff becomes fourth President of the Church
24 September 1890	Wilford Woodruff issues the "Manifesto"
6 April 1893	Wilford Woodruff dedicates the Salt Lake Temple
28 March 1895	Birth of Spencer W. Kimball, Salt Lake City
24 April 1898	Spain declares war on the United States, and the Spanish-American War begins
2 September 1898	Death of Wilford Woodruff, San Francisco, California
13 September 1898	Lorenzo Snow becomes fifth President of the Church
28 March 1899	Birth of Harold B. Lee, Clifton, Idaho
8 May 1899	Lorenzo Snow announces renewed emphasis on tithing
4 August 1899	Birth of Ezra Taft Benson, Whitney, Idaho
10 October 1901	Death of Lorenzo Snow, Salt Lake City
17 October 1901	Joseph F. Smith becomes sixth President of the Church
17 December 1903	Wright Brothers make 59-second flight at Kitty Hawk
Summer 1906	Joseph F. Smith becomes first Church President to visit Europe
14 November 1907	Birth of Howard W. Hunter, Boise, Idaho
23 June 1910	Birth of Gordon B. Hinckley, Salt Lake City
28 July 1914	World War I begins
11 November 1918	Armistice signed, ending World War I
19 November 1918	Death of Joseph F. Smith, Salt Lake City
23 November 1918	Heber J. Grant becomes seventh President of the Church

27 November 1919	Heber J. Grant dedicates Hawaii Temple, first outside the United States
1 September 1939	Germany invades Poland, beginning World War II
7 December 1941	Japanese bomb Pearl Harbor
8 May 1945	Germany surrenders (V-E Day)
14 May 1945	Death of Heber J. Grant, Salt Lake City
21 May 1945	George Albert Smith becomes eighth President of the Church
14 August 1945	Japan surrenders (V-J Day)
3 November 1945	George Albert Smith meets with U.S. President Harry S. Truman and discusses Church plan to send relief to Europe
1947	Church membership reaches one million
25 June 1950	North Korea's surprise invasion of South Korea begins Korean War
4 April 1951	Death of George Albert Smith, Salt Lake City
9 April 1951	David O. McKay becomes ninth President of the Church
27 July 1953	Korean War ends as armistice is signed
3 December 1962	First Spanish-speaking stake organized, in Mexico City
22 November 1963	John F. Kennedy assassinated in Dallas, Texas
January 1965	Family home evening program is implemented
7 March 1965	First U.S. ground combat troops arrive in Vietnam
18 January 1970	Death of David O. McKay, Salt Lake City
23 January 1970	Joseph Fielding Smith becomes tenth President of the Church
27 August 1971	First area conference of the Church held in Manchester, England
2 July 1972	Death of Joseph Fielding Smith, Salt Lake City
7 July 1972	Harold B. Lee becomes eleventh President of the Church
28 January 1973	Cease-fire agreement reached in Vietnam
8 March 1973	First stake on mainland Asia organized in Seoul, Korea
26 December 1973	Death of Harold B. Lee, Salt Lake City

30 December 1973	Spencer W. Kimball becomes twelfth President of the Church
30 April 1975	South Vietnam falls to the Communists
9 June 1978	First Presidency announces revelation that all worthy males are now eligible to receive the priesthood
5 November 1985	Death of Spencer W. Kimball, Salt Lake City
10 November 1985	Ezra Taft Benson becomes thirteenth President of the Church
15 May 1988	The Aba Nigeria Stake organized, the first in West Africa
30 May 1994	Death of Ezra Taft Benson, Salt Lake City
5 June 1994	Howard W. Hunter becomes fourteenth President of the Church
11 December 1994	The Mexico City Mexico Contretras Stake organized, the 2,000th in the Church
3 March 1995	Death of Howard W. Hunter, Salt Lake City
12 March 1995	Gordon B. Hinckley becomes fifteenth President of the Church
27 May 1996	Gordon B. Hinckley becomes first Church president to visit mainland China
1997	Church membership reaches 10 million
1 April 2000	The first general conference to be held in the new Conference Center is convened
6 April 2000	On the 170th anniversary of the founding of the Church, Gordon B. Hinckley dedicates the Palmyra New York Temple
September 2001	For the first time, the Church has more non-English-speaking members than those who speak English
11 September 2001	Terrorists hijack four airliners, crashing them into the World Trade Center, the Pentagon, and a field in Pennsylvania. Thousands are killed, including five members of the Church
27 June 2002	Gordon B. Hinckley dedicates the Nauvoo Illinois Temple on the 158th anniversary of the deaths of Joseph and Hyrum Smith; it is the 113th operating temple in the Church

NOTES

Notes to Introduction

1. Brown, *An Abundant Life*, 15–16.
2. Ibid., 15.

Notes to Chapter 1: Joseph Smith

1. *Millennial Star* 13 (15 November 1851): 339.
2. Smith, *History of the Church*, 3:304.
3. Ibid., 5:498.
4. Joseph Smith to James Arlington Bennett, 8 September 1842, in Smith, *Personal Writings of Joseph Smith*, 575–76. Bennett was baptized in 1843 and was Joseph Smith's first choice as vice-presidential running mate in 1844, though Bennett declined.
5. Smith, *History of the Church*, 5:340–41, 344. Pelatiah Brown remained faithful. In January of 1845, Brigham Young called him to preside over a branch of the Church. He was also appointed to collect donations for the Nauvoo Temple (*Times and Seasons* 6 [January 1845]). In 1846, as William Clayton was going west with his family, he hired Pelatiah Brown as a teamster. One day Brother Brown went swimming when he was supposed to be working. Concluding that Pelatiah "will not work only when he has a mind to," William Clayton asked him to seek employment elsewhere (Clayton, *William Clayton's Journal*, 57). I have found no further record of Pelatiah Brown.
6. Arrington, *Presidents of the Church*, 28.
7. Alexander, *Things in Heaven and Earth*, 31.
8. Andrus, *Joseph Smith*, 22–23.

9. Ibid., 23.
10. Ibid.
11. Ibid., 23–24.
11. Arrington, *Presidents of the Church*, 29–30.

NOTES TO CHAPTER 2: BRIGHAM YOUNG

1. Young, *Letters of Brigham Young to His Sons*, 222.
2. Young, *Discourses of Brigham Young*, 232.
3. Ibid.
4. Ibid.
5. Ibid.
6. *Journal of Discourses*, 10:97.
7. Arrington, *Presidents of the Church*, 47.
8. Gates, *Life Story of Brigham Young*, 367.
9. Arrington, *Brigham Young: American Moses*, 217.
10. Ibid., 216.
11. Ibid., 220.
12. Nibley, *Brigham Young, the Man and His Work*, 183.
13. Arrington, *Brigham Young: American Moses*, 221.
14. Ibid.
15. Ibid., 4.

NOTES TO CHAPTER 3: JOHN TAYLOR

1. *Journal of Discourses*, 8:100.
2. Ibid., 23:63.
3. Ibid., 24:36–37; some paragraphing added for readability.
4. Ibid., 21:16; some paragraphing added for readability.
5. Arrington, *Presidents of the Church*, 81.
6. Roberts, *Life of John Taylor*, 32–33.
7. Arrington, *Presidents of the Church*, 111–12.

NOTES TO CHAPTER 4: WILFORD WOODRUFF

1. Woodruff, *Discourses of Wilford Woodruff*, 293–94.
2. Ibid., 276.
3. Ibid., 276–77.
4. Ibid., 277.
5. Ibid., 61.
6. Ibid.
7. Ibid., 61–62.
8. Ibid., 62.
9. Ibid.

10. Cowley, *Wilford Woodruff*, 116–19.
11. Woodruff, *Discourses of Wilford Woodruff*, 293.

NOTES TO CHAPTER 5: LORENZO SNOW

1. Stuy, *Collected Discourses*, 5:451–52.
2. Ludlow, *Latter-day Prophets Speak*, 15.
3. Ibid., 16.
4. Arrington, *Presidents of the Church*, 152.
5. Ibid., 152–53.
6. Romney, *Life of Lorenzo Snow*, 66–67.
7. Snow, *Biography and Family Record of Lorenzo Snow*, 232.
8. See ibid., 276–81.
9. See Van Wagoner and Walker, *A Book of Mormons*, 335–36.
10. Snow, "The Redeemer Appears to President Lorenzo Snow," 139–41.
11. Ibid., 141.
12. Stuy, *Collected Discourses*, 5:451.

NOTES TO CHAPTER 6: JOSEPH F. SMITH

1. Smith, *Life of Joseph F. Smith*, 4.
2. Smith, *Gospel Doctrine*, 281–82, 316.
3. Ibid., 318.
4. Ibid., 316–17.
5. Ibid., 317–18.
6. Ibid., 314–15.
7. Joseph F. Smith to Samuel L. Adams, 11 May 1888, in McConkie, *Truth and Courage*, 6.
8. Smith, *Life of Joseph F. Smith*, 185–86.
9. Ibid., 421.
10. Joseph F. Smith to Emily and Edith Smith, 22 May 1915. Original in possession of John William Walker family. Emily Jane Smith was born on 11 September 1888. She married John William Walker on 5 May 1918. She died on 12 December 1982.
11. Joseph F. Smith to Emily Smith, 8 March 1918. Original in possession of the Walker family. Thanks to Edith Walker LeCheminant and J. Douglas LeCheminant, daughter and grandson of Emily Jane Smith Walker, for assisting me with my research on Joseph F. Smith and for giving their kind permission to use this letter and the card listed in the previous note.

NOTES TO CHAPTER 7: HEBER J. GRANT

1. Grant, *Gospel Standards*, 259.
2. Grant, "In the Hour of Parting," 330.

3. Heber J. Grant to Anthony and Elizabeth Ivins, 18 February 1880, Utah State Historical Society.

4. Grant, *Gospel Standards*, 364–66.

5. Hinckley, *Heber J. Grant: Highlights in the Life of a Great Leader*, 205–6.

6. Heber J. Grant to Elizabeth Snow Ivins, 17 October 1934, Utah State Historical Society.

NOTES TO CHAPTER 8: GEORGE ALBERT SMITH

1. Smith, *Teachings of George Albert Smith*, 138–39.

2. Dedicatory prayer, Idaho Falls Temple, 23 September 1945; cited in Bowen, *Church Welfare Plan*, 67.

3. In Conference Report, October 1949, 170–72.

4. In Conference Report, October 1947, 5–6.

5. Rudd, *Pure Religion*, 247–48.

6. Kimball and Kimball, *Spencer W. Kimball*, 237–38.

7. In Conference Report, October 1947, 19–20.

NOTES TO CHAPTER 9: DAVID O. MCKAY

1. Anderson, *Prophets I Have Known*, 133–34.

2. McKay, *Pathways to Happiness*, 159.

3. McKay, *Gospel Ideals*, 253–54.

4. Hinckley, "An Appreciation of Stephen L Richards," 498.

5. Ibid., 499.

6. Anderson, *Prophets I Have Known*, 144.

7. Ibid., 140.

8. In Conference Report, April 1951, 157.

9. Ibid., 150–51.

10. Ibid., 154–55.

11. Anderson, *Prophets I Have Known*, 145.

12. Ibid.

13. Ibid., 146.

14. McKay, *Home Memories of President David O. McKay*, 40.

15. Ibid., 41.

16. Ibid., 45.

17. Hugh J. Cannon, "The Chinese Realm Dedicated for the Preaching of the Gospel," 443, 445.

18. In Conference Report, April 1922, 65.

19. McKay, *Cherished Experiences from the Writings of David O. McKay*, 51–52.

20. Morrell, *Highlights in the Life of David O. McKay*, 69.

21. McKay, *Home Memories of President David O. McKay*, 69.

22. *Church History in the Fulness of Times*, 501.

23. McKay, *Home Memories of President David O. McKay*, 58.
24. In Conference Report, April 1922, 62.
25. Garr, Cannon, and Cowan, *Encyclopedia of Latter-day Saint History*, 726–27.

NOTES TO CHAPTER 10: JOSEPH FIELDING SMITH

1. McConkie, *True and Faithful*, 70–71.
2. Smith, *Answers to Gospel Questions*, 4:156–57.
3. In Conference Report, October 1947, 147–48.
4. Smith and Stewart, *Life of Joseph Fielding Smith*, 287.
5. Ibid., 287–88.
6. Ibid., 288.
7. Ibid., 252.
8. Ibid., 259.
9. In Conference Report, April 1972, 163–64.
10. Smith and Stewart, *Life of Joseph Fielding Smith*, 375–77; emphasis added.

NOTES TO CHAPTER 11: HAROLD B. LEE

1. Lee, *Teachings of Harold B. Lee*, 614.
2. Ibid., 615.
3. Ibid., 619–20.
4. Ibid., 620
5. Ibid.
6. Ibid.
7. Goates, *Harold B. Lee*, 481.
8. Ibid., 483–84.
9. Ibid., 484–86, 490.
10. Arrington, *Presidents of the Church*, 355–56.

NOTES TO CHAPTER 12: SPENCER W. KIMBALL

1. Kimball, *Teachings of Spencer W. Kimball*, 38–39.
2. Ibid., 167–68.
3. Ibid., 168.
4. Ibid., 124.
5. Ibid., 123.
6. Ibid., 123–24.
7. Ibid., 122.
8. Lindsay, "Ye Have Done It unto Me," 15.
9. Adapted from Miner and Kimball, *Camilla*, 182–84.
10. Maxwell, "Spencer, the Beloved: Leader-Servant," 8, 10–13.

NOTES TO CHAPTER 13: EZRA TAFT BENSON

1. Dew, *Ezra Taft Benson*, 296.
2. Benson, *Teachings of Ezra Taft Benson*, 330.
3. Ibid.
4. Ibid., 331.
5. Ibid., 460.
6. Ibid.
7. Ibid., 461.
8. Ibid.
9. Ibid.
10. Eisenhower had defeated the Democratic candidate, Adlai Stevenson, by a wide margin: 442 electoral votes to 89.
11. Adapted from Dew, *Ezra Taft Benson*, 253–91.
12. Ibid., 505–7.

NOTES TO CHAPTER 14: HOWARD W. HUNTER

1. Knowles, *Howard W. Hunter*, 204.
2. Hunter, *That We Might Have Joy*, 147.
3. Hunter, *Teachings of Howard W. Hunter*, 73.
4. Ibid., 97–98.
5. Huntsman, "A Remarkable and Selfless Life," 24–25.
6. Holland, "Miracles of the Restoration," 32.
7. Knowles, *Howard W. Hunter*, 303.

NOTES TO CHAPTER 15: GORDON B. HINCKLEY

1. Dew, *Go Forward with Faith*, 488.
2. Hinckley, *Teachings of Gordon B. Hinckley*, 704.
3. Ibid., 705.
4. Flake, *Prophets and Apostles of the Last Dispensation*, 457–58.
5. Gordon B. Hinckley to Joseph F. Merrill, 21 August 1935, L. Tom Perry Special Collections Library, Harold B. Lee Library, Brigham Young University.
6. Joseph F. Merrill to Gordon B. Hinckley, 23 August 1935, L. Tom Perry Special Collections Library.
7. Dew, *Go Forward with Faith*, 84.
8. Ibid., 85.
9. Ibid., 511.
10. Ibid., 516.
11. Ibid., 547.
12. Ibid., 555.
13. Ibid., 547–48.
14. Ibid., 554–55.

BIBLIOGRAPHY

Alexander, Thomas G. *Things in Heaven and Earth: The Life and Times of Wilford Woodruff, a Mormon Prophet*. Salt Lake City: Signature Books, 1991.

Allen, James B. and Glen M. Leonard. *The Story of the Latter-day Saints*. Salt Lake City: Deseret Book, 1976, 1992.

Anderson, Joseph. *Prophets I Have Known*. Salt Lake City: Deseret Book, 1973.

Andrus, Hyrum L. *Joseph Smith, the Man and the Seer*. Salt Lake City: Deseret Book, 1960.

Andrus, Hyrum L., and Helen Mae Andrus. *They Knew the Prophet*. Salt Lake City: Bookcraft, 1974.

Arrington, Leonard J. *Brigham Young: American Moses*. Urbana and Chicago: University of Illinois Press, 1986.

———. *The Presidents of the Church*. Salt Lake City: Deseret Book, 1986.

Babbel, Frederick W. *On Wings of Faith: Ezra Taft Benson Takes Church Welfare Supplies into War-torn Europe*. Salt Lake City: Bookcraft, 1972.

Bennett, Richard E. *We'll Find the Place: The Mormon Exodus, 1846–1848*. Salt Lake City: Deseret Book, 1997.

Benson, Ezra Taft. *The Teachings of Ezra Taft Benson*. Salt Lake City: Bookcraft, 1988.

Bowen, Albert E. *Church Welfare Plan*. Salt Lake City: Deseret Sunday School Union, 1946.

Brown, Hugh B. *An Abundant Life: The Memoirs of Hugh B. Brown*. Edited by Edwin B. Firmage. Salt Lake City: Signature Books, 1999.

Cannon, Hugh J. "The Chinese Realm Dedicated for the Preaching of the Gospel," *Improvement Era* 24 (March 1921): 443–45.

Church History in the Fulness of Times: The History of The Church of Jesus Christ of Latter-day Saints. Prepared by the Church Educational System for Religion Courses 341–43. Salt Lake City: The Church of Jesus Christ of Latter-day Saints, 1989.

Clayton, William. *William Clayton's Journal: A Daily Record of the Journey of the Original Company of Mormon Pioneers from Nauvoo, Illinois, to the Valley of the Great Salt Lake*. Salt Lake City: Deseret News, 1921.

Cowley, Matthias F. *Wilford Woodruff: History of His Life and Labors*. Salt Lake City: Bookcraft, 1964.

Deseret News 2003 Church Almanac. Salt Lake City: The Church of Jesus Christ of Latter-day Saints, 2002.

Dew, Sheri L. *Ezra Taft Benson: A Biography*. Salt Lake City: Deseret Book, 1987, 1989.

———. *Go Forward with Faith: The Biography of Gordon B. Hinckley*. Salt Lake City: Deseret Book, 1996.

Flake, Lawrence R. *Prophets and Apostles of the Last Dispensation*. Provo, Utah: BYU Religious Studies Center, 2001.

Garr, Arnold K., Donald Q. Cannon, and Richard O. Cowan. *Encyclopedia of Latter-day Saint History*. Salt Lake City: Deseret Book, 2000.

Gates, Susa Young, in collaboration with Leah D. Widtsoe. *The Life Story of Brigham Young*. New York: Macmillan, 1931.

Gibbons, Francis M. *Dynamic Disciples, Prophets of God*. Salt Lake City: Deseret Book, 1996.

———. *George Albert Smith: Kind and Caring Christian, Prophet of God*. Salt Lake City: Deseret Book, 1990.

———. *Heber J. Grant: Man of Steel, Prophet of God*. Salt Lake City: Deseret Book, 1979.

Goates, L. Brent. *Harold B. Lee: Prophet and Seer*. Salt Lake City: Bookcraft, 1985.

Grant, Heber J. *Gospel Standards: Selections from the Sermons and Writings of Heber J. Grant*. Compiled by G. Homer Durham. Salt Lake City: Improvement Era, 1981.

———. "In the Hour of Parting." *Improvement Era* 43 (June 1940): 330, 383.

Heslop, J. M., and Dell R. Van Orden. *Joseph Fielding Smith: A Prophet among the People*. Salt Lake City: Deseret Book, 1971.

Hinckley, Bryant S. *Heber J. Grant: Highlights in the Life of a Great Leader*. Salt Lake City: Deseret Book, 1951.

Hinckley, Gordon B. "An Appreciation of Stephen L Richards." *Improvement Era* 54 (July 1951): 496–99, 514.

———. *Teachings of Gordon B. Hinckley*. Salt Lake City: Deseret Book, 1997.

Holland, Jeffrey R. "Miracles of the Restoration." *Ensign*, November 1994, 31–34.

Holzapfel, Richard Neitzel, and R. Q. Shupe. *Joseph F. Smith: Portrait of a Prophet*. Salt Lake City: Deseret Book, 2000.

Hunter, Howard W. *The Teachings of Howard W. Hunter*. Edited by Clyde J. Williams. Salt Lake City: Deseret Book, 1997.

———. *That We Might Have Joy*. Salt Lake City: Deseret Book, 1994.

Huntsman, Jon M. "A Remarkable and Selfless Life." *Ensign*, April 1995, 24–25.

Jenson, Andrew. *LDS Biographical Encyclopedia*. 4 vols. Salt Lake City: Andrew Jenson Historical Company, 1901–1936.

Journal of Discourses. 26 vols. London: Latter-day Saints' Book Depot, 1854–1886.

Kimball, Edward L., and Andrew E. Kimball. *Spencer W. Kimball: Twelfth President of The Church of Jesus Christ of Latter-day Saints*. Salt Lake City: Bookcraft, 1977.

Kimball, Spencer W. *The Teachings of Spencer W. Kimball, Twelfth President of The Church of Jesus Christ of Latter-day Saints*. Edited by Edward L. Kimball. Salt Lake City: Bookcraft, 1982.

Knowles, Eleanor. *Howard W. Hunter*. Salt Lake City: Deseret Book, 1994.

Lee, Harold B. *The Teachings of Harold B. Lee.* Edited by Clyde J. Williams. Salt Lake City: Bookcraft, 1996.

Lindsay, Richard P. "Ye Have Done It unto Me." *Ensign,* May 1990, 14–15.

Ludlow, Daniel H., ed. *Encyclopedia of Mormonism.* 4 vols. New York: Macmillan, 1992.

———. *Latter-day Prophets Speak: Selections from the Sermons and Writings of Church Presidents.* Salt Lake City: Bookcraft, 1948, 1988.

Madsen, Truman G. *Joseph Smith the Prophet.* Salt Lake City: Bookcraft, 1989.

Maxwell, Neal A. "Spencer, the Beloved: Leader-Servant." *Ensign,* December 1985, 8–19.

McConkie, Joseph Fielding. *True and Faithful.* Salt Lake City: Bookcraft, 1971.

———, ed. *Truth and Courage: Joseph F. Smith Letters.* N.p., 1998.

McKay, David O. *Cherished Experiences from the Writings of David O. McKay.* Compiled by Clare Middlemiss. Salt Lake City: Deseret Book, 1955.

———. *Gospel Ideals: Selections from the Discourses of David O. McKay.* Salt Lake City: Improvement Era, 1953.

———. *Man May Know for Himself: Teachings of President David O. McKay.* Compiled by Clare Middlemiss. Salt Lake City: Deseret Book, 1967.

———. *Pathways to Happiness.* Compiled by Llewelyn R. McKay. Salt Lake City: Bookcraft, 1957.

McKay, Llewelyn R., comp. *Home Memories of President David O. McKay.* Salt Lake City: Deseret Book, 1956.

Miner, Caroline Eyring, and Edward L. Kimball. *Camilla: A Biography of Camilla Eyring Kimball.* Salt Lake City: Deseret Book, 1980.

Morrell, Jeanette McKay. *Highlights in the Life of David O. McKay.* Salt Lake City: Deseret Book, 1966.

Morris, Larry E. *And Now You Know: The Rest of the Story from the Lives of Well-Known Latter-day Saints.* Salt Lake City: Deseret Book, 2002.

———. *A Treasury of Latter-day Saint Letters.* Salt Lake City: Deseret Book, 2001.

Nibley, Preston. *Brigham Young, the Man and His Work.* Salt Lake City: Deseret News Press, 1936.

Parry, Jay A., and Larry E. Morris. *The Mormon Book of Lists.* Salt Lake City: Bookcraft, 1987.

The Presidents of the Church: An Outline for Institute of Religion Instructors. Provo, Utah: The Church of Jesus Christ of Latter-day Saints Church Schools, 1968.

Pusey, Merlo J. *Builders of the Kingdom: George A. Smith, John Henry Smith, George Albert Smith.* Provo, Utah: Brigham Young University Press, 1981.

Roberts, B. H. *A Comprehensive History of The Church of Jesus Christ of Latter-day Saints, Century One.* 6 vols. Salt Lake City: The Church of Jesus Christ of Latter-day Saints, 1930.

———. *The Life of John Taylor, Third President of The Church of Jesus Christ of Latter-day Saints.* Salt Lake City: George Q. Cannon & Sons, 1892.

Romney, Thomas C. *The Life of Lorenzo Snow, Fifth President of The Church of Jesus Christ of Latter-day Saints.* Salt Lake City: Sugarhouse Press, 1955.

Rudd, Glenn L. *Pure Religion: The Story of Church Welfare Since 1930.* Salt Lake City: The Church of Jesus Christ of Latter-day Saints, 1995.

Smith, George Albert. *The Teachings of George Albert Smith.* Edited by Robert McIntosh and Susan McIntosh. Salt Lake City: Bookcraft, 1996.

Smith, Joseph. *History of The Church of Jesus Christ of Latter-day Saints.* Edited by B. H. Roberts. 7 vols. 2d ed. rev. Salt Lake City: The Church of Jesus Christ of Latter-day Saints, 1948.

———. *The Papers of Joseph Smith.* Edited by Dean C. Jessee. 2 vols. Salt Lake City: Deseret Book, 1989, 1992.

———. *Personal Writings of Joseph Smith.* Edited by Dean C. Jessee. Revised edition. Salt Lake City: Deseret Book, 2002.

———. *Scriptural Teachings of the Prophet Joseph Smith.* Selected and arranged by Joseph Fielding Smith; scriptural annotations and introduction by Richard C. Galbraith. Salt Lake City: Deseret Book, 1993.

Smith, Joseph F. *Gospel Doctrine.* Compiled by John A. Widtsoe. 5th ed. Salt Lake City: Deseret Book, 1966.

Smith, Joseph Fielding. *Answers to Gospel Questions.* 5 vols. Salt Lake City: Deseret Book, 1957–1966.

———. *Life of Joseph F. Smith.* Salt Lake City: Deseret Book, 1969.

Smith, Joseph Fielding, Jr., and John J. Stewart. *The Life of Joseph Fielding Smith.* Salt Lake City: Deseret Book, 1972.

Snow, Eliza R. *Biography and Family Record of Lorenzo Snow.* Salt Lake City: Deseret News Company, 1884.

Snow, Leroi C. "The Redeemer Appears to President Lorenzo Snow." *The Deseret News,* 2 April 1938; in *Temples of the Most High.* Compiled by N. B. Lundwall. Salt Lake City: Bookcraft, 1968, 139–42.

Stuy, Brian H., ed., *Collected Discourses,* 5 vols. Burbank, Calif., and Woodland Hills, Utah: B.H.S. Publishing, 1987–1992.

Taylor, John. *The Gospel Kingdom: Selections from the Writings and Discourses of John Taylor.* Compiled by G. Homer Durham. Salt Lake City: Bookcraft, 1987, 1990.

Taylor, Samuel W. *The Last Pioneer: John Taylor, a Mormon Prophet.* Salt Lake City: Signature Books, 1999.

Teachings of Presidents of the Church: John Taylor. Salt Lake City: The Church of Jesus Christ of Latter-day Saints, 2001.

Todd, Jay M. "President Howard W. Hunter: Fourteenth President of the Church." *Ensign,* July 1994, 4–5.

Van Wagoner, Richard S., and Steven C. Walker. *A Book of Mormons.* Salt Lake City: Signature Books, 1982.

Wetterau, Bruce. *The New York Public Library Book of Chronologies.* New York: Prentice Hall, 1990.

Woodruff, Wilford. *The Discourses of Wilford Woodruff.* Compiled by G. Homer Durham. Salt Lake City: Bookcraft, 1946, 1990.

Young, Brigham. *Discourses of Brigham Young.* Compiled by John A. Widtsoe. Salt Lake City: Deseret Book, 1954.

———. *Letters of Brigham Young to His Sons.* Edited by Dean C. Jessee. Salt Lake City: Deseret Book, 1974.

INDEX

for children, 39–41; Ezra Taft Benson on the roles of parents, 112–14

Fife, William S. and Lois, Joseph Fielding Smith letter to, 80–81

First principles, Joseph Smith on declaring, 4

Flake, Lawrence R., 124

Free agency, John Taylor on, 14–15

Friendship, David O. McKay on the value of, 63–64

Galbraith, David B., 91, 92

Garden Tomb, 91–92

Gates, Susa Young, 10–11

Goates, L. Brent, 91–92

Grant, Augusta Winters, 53

Grant, Daniel Wells, 50

Grant, Heber J.: on the Church's financial condition at the time of Wilford Woodruff's death, 35; on finding comfort in the death of a loved one, 48–49; letter to Anthony W. and Elizabeth Ivins on the death of their son, 49–50; dreams about son Heber's death, 50–51; on the death of son Heber, 51–52; Lucy Grant on meeting recipients of books from, 52; letter to Elizabeth Ivins on the death of Anthony W., 52–53; biographical sketch of, 53; meets with Gordon B. Hinckley to discuss need for good Church literature in mission field, 125–26

Grant, Heber Stringham, 50–52

Grant, Lucy, 52

Gratitude, Joseph Fielding Smith on, 82–83

Great Britain, missionary journey of Wilford Woodruff to, 23–27

Greeley, Horace, 12–13

Harvey, Paul, 113

Hinckley, Gordon B.: on the friendship between Stephen L Richards and David O. McKay, 65; journeys to Holy Land with Harold B. Lee, 88–94;

reorganizes London Stake presidency, 89; rededicates Greece for preaching of the gospel, 91; speaks at Garden Tomb meeting, 92; on Holy Land journey with Harold B. Lee, 93–94; Thomas S. Monson on, 122; on the virtue of work, 123; serves under Joseph F. Merrill in European mission, 124–25; meets with Church leaders to discuss need for good Church literature in mission field, 125–26; accepts position as executive secretary of Church Radio, Publicity, and Mission Literature Committee, 126–27; on being ordained Church President, 127; Boyd K. Packer on, 127; Joseph B. Wirthlin on, 127; sustained as Assistant to the Twelve and as apostle, 127; rigorous schedule of, 127–28; biographical sketch of, 128; Marjorie P. Hinckley on, 128

Hinckley, Marjorie P., 128

Holland, Jeffrey R., on Howard W. Hunter, 119–21

Holy Land, visit of Harold B. Lee and Gordon B. Hinckley to, 88–94

Honesty, Brigham Young on, 8–10

Hope, Bob, 109–10

Hunter, Howard W.: honored by Ninth Circuit Court of Appeals, 115; on compassion, 116; on God's love for all of his children, 116–17; Jon M. Huntsman on, 117–19; Jeffrey R. Holland on, 119–21; biographical sketch of, 121; visits Saints in Russia, 121

Huntsman, Jon M., on Howard W. Hunter, 117–19

Hyde, Orson, 91

Idaho Falls Idaho Temple, George Albert Smith dedicatory prayer for, 55

Indians. See Native Americans

Ingratitude, Joseph Fielding Smith on the sin of, 78–79

Inspiration. See Revelation